Bank Finance for Companies

by

Robert R. Pennington, LL.D., (B'ham)

Professor of Commercial Law at the University of Birmingham,
Solicitor of the Supreme Court of England

London
Sweet & Maxwell
Centre for Commercial Law Studies
1987

Published in 1987 by
Sweet & Maxwell Ltd. of
11 New Fetter Lane, London
Computerset by Promenade Graphics Limited, Cheltenham
and printed in Great Britain by
Thomson Litho Limited
East Kilbride, Scotland

British Library Cataloguing in Publication Data
Pennington, R.R.
  Bank finance for companies.
  1. Corporations—Great Britain—Finance
  2. Bank loans—Great Britain
  I. Title
  332. 1'753   HG4135

  ISBN 0–421–38490–5

Foreword

Every year for the past five years the Centre for Commercial Law Studies at Queen Mary College has organised a series of lectures, the Commercial Law Lectures, in which a single speaker examines in detail some aspect of commercial law of topical interest and importance. Each set of lectures, after revision and expansion, has been published as a book by the Centre and Sweet & Maxwell, and has clearly satisfied a strong demand, both in this country and overseas.

It gives me particular pleasure to welcome the appearance of the fifth publication in the series, *Bank Finance for Companies*, which reproduces the revised version of the Commercial Law Lectures 1987, delivered by that distinguished academic writer, Professor Robert Pennington, of Birmingham University. Bob Pennington's knowledge of commercial law is encyclopedic. A lecturer of international repute and the author of a standard textbook on company law, now in its fifth edition, he is equally at home in many other areas of law, and has published and lectured in such disparate fields as partnership, stannaries, patents, banking, securities regulation and electronic dealings in money and securities.

Bank Finance for Companies provides an intergated description and legal analysis of the principal forms of corporate finance extended by banks and their subsidiaries. The subject is vast, but Professor Pennington succeeds not only in containing it within manageable compass but also in offering penetrating new insights into some familiar problems. No one interested in bank financing of companies, whether as a lawyer, a banker or a company seeking bank finance, can fail to derive benefit from this new publication.

Centre for Commercial Law Studies,　　　　　　　　　　Roy Goode
Queen Mary College,
August, 1987.

Preface

It is a commonplace that the services provided by banks have undergone a near revolution during the last fifteen years. The services provided for consumers have expanded enormously (credit cards, credit transfers, direct debits and electronic money transfers) and, correspondingly, the banks have widened the services they provide for companies which seek to raise share or loan capital, in order to finance their undertakings. This has been largely facilitated by the acquisition or establishment by the commercial banks, of subsidiary companies providing specialist commercial services ranging from leasing and hire purchase facilities to the marketing of traditional securities in the manner formally exclusively undertaken by the merchant banks.

A survey of the present facilities provided by the banks for the raising of finance by companies, therefore covers a very wide area, and in this book an account is given of the various different forms of the facilities which the banks now offer. The traditional forms of financing by way of bank overdraft and short and medium fixed term loans, occupy the first Chapter of the book, and in the second Chapter the various other forms of financing concerned with loans and advances, are examined. After a consideration of the enforcement of claims by banks against companies which they have financed, the fourth Chapter concerns the special position of bank financing of groups of companies. Finally, the fifth Chapter examines the more novel forms of bank financing which have appeared during the last ten years, and contains a prognosis of likely developments in this respect, in the future.

The subject of bank financing of companies, looked at from the legal point of view has, in the past usually involved a segmentation of the subject and its treatment under various different rubrics, comprising partly banking law, partly company law and partly the law and practice of the financial markets. The purpose of this book is to draw these different threads together and to treat the subject of the legal aspects of bank finance for companies as an integrated whole. In view of the recent developments in banking services and practices, this is undoubtedly the manner in which the subject will have to be treated in future.

University of Birmingham
November, 1987

vii

Contents

Table of Cases

Coventry University

Lanchester Library

25/10/2023 15:09:32

Return Receipt

1. Central banking and banking regulation /
38001002404212
returned

2. Bank finance for companies /
38001000912877
returned

3. The banking crisis handbook /
38001005880491
returned

Thank you for using this service

Table of Statutory Instruments

Rules of the Supreme Court

R.S.C. (Revision) 1965 (S.I. 1965 No. 1776)

I

Bank Loans to Companies for General Purposes

The forms and techniques employed by the banks to finance the operations of companies have undergone a revolution during the last 15 years. The traditional overdraft facility has been extensively replaced by the term loan for periods between two and 10 years or even longer, and the range and character of the securities which banks take to ensure that they are well placed if the borrower collapses financially have been radically elaborated. The process of change has not yet reached a conclusion. New forms of financing or variations on existing forms are constantly appearing. Probably the most important of these is the acceptance of equity participations in borrowing companies, a phenomenon which the traditional banker of 1960 would have regarded as anathema. It is true that such participations, or options to subscribe for or to convert loans into equity securities, are usually part of financing transactions negotiated by the commercial banks' merchant banking subsidiaries rather than by the banks themselves, but this is a distinction without a difference. The banks' subsidiaries are all 100 per cent. owned by one or more commercial banks, and are treated, like their leasing, factoring and overseas loans subsidiaries merely as departments of a whole, integrated enterprise.

Overdrafts and term loans

In this first Chapter the various forms of loan facilities which banks at present make available to companies for their general purposes will be surveyed. The overdraft facility undoubtedly still predominates among these facilities, not only in terms of volume, but also because it is the facility which is used by all companies, from the largest public company with a Stock Exchange listing for its shares to the smallest private company formed to run a small business and having only a handful of shareholders. The term loan repayable over three, four or five years has, however, become a serious rival to the overdraft in recent years. It offers the assurance that unless the borrowing company defaults in making the periodic payments of interest and repayments of capital called for by the loan agreement, the loan cannot be called in before the contractual date for repayment in the way an overdraft repayable on demand may be. Furthermore,

1

the rate of interest payable on a term loan, although variable in the same way as overdraft interest, is often more favourable to the borrower than the rates charged for overdraft interest. This is because term loan interest is related to current market interest rates over a substantial time, usually three or six months, whereas overdraft interest may change from day to day.

During the last 10 years the commercial banks have made term loans to financially sound companies for longer periods than hitherto, and medium-sized and large companies may now borrow from the banks for seven or 10 years or even longer. These medium or long term loans have to a large extent replaced the loans at fixed rates of interest which public companies used to raise by offers of their debentures and loan stock to the public for subscription. Debenture issues by prospectus all but disappeared during the economic recession of the 1970s, largely because of the kaleidoscopic changes in interest rates, as well as the generally pessimistic market outlook. The banks have stepped in to fill the gap, and have solved the problem of fluctuating market interest rates by making medium and long-term loans at interest rates which vary with the current level of market rates.

Specialised forms of bank finance

In addition to loan finance in the strict sense, banks or more usually their specialised subsidiaries formed for the purpose, have over the last 15 years provided finance for companies in ways which do not explicitly involve loans. Examples of these facilities are the financing of companies' acquisitions of plant and machinery by hiring and hire purchase arrangements, the factoring or discounting of trade debts owed to companies by their customers, and lease-back transactions by which companies realise the current value of their freehold or long leasehold properties by selling them for cash and taking in return a lease of the properties at a full commercial rent from the purchasers. Also banks have continued to finance import and export transactions by issuing letters of credit or guarantees, and they and their subsidiaries have provided short term financing facilities by accepting or discounting bills of exchange, promissory notes and sterling commercial notes. These specialised forms of financing will be considered in the second and fifth Chapters of this book.

1. BANK FINANCING BY OVERDRAFT

Any detailed examination of bank lending must begin with the overdraft. Technically an overdraft is a fact, not a transaction. It arises when a customer of a bank draws on his current account so extensively that he eliminates any credit balance he has and produces a negative balance. The legal relationship of bank and customer has long been held by the courts to be that of debtor and creditor while the account is in credit,[1] and so when a current account is overdrawn, the roles of the parties are reversed, and the customer becomes the debtor of the bank for the amount overdrawn. When the customer later pays amounts into the credit of his account or when amounts are paid into it with his express or implied authority (*e.g.* by credit transfer), the overdraft is reduced or eliminated, and the customer's indebtedness to the bank is *pro tanto* or completely discharged.

Overdraft facilities

The interesting point to notice is that these changes in the legal position of the parties may take place without any express agreement between them. Whether they occur because of the particular relationship between the parties (*i.e.* that of bank and customer), or whether it is implied as a term of the contract between the bank and its customer when the latter's account is opened, is of no practical significance. What is important, however, is the rule that a customer is not entitled to overdraw on his account as of right; this is because the bank's indebtedness to its customer is eliminated when he draws out the whole of the credit balance on his account, and there is no further indebtedness of the bank on which he can draw. Consequently, in the absence of a contrary agreement, the bank may refuse to pay any further amounts to the customer, or to honour cheques drawn by him, or to undertake obligations to make payments to third parties at the customer's request (*e.g.* to accept bills of exchange drawn by the customer, or to issue letters of credit to persons to whom the customer has or will incur indebtedness). However, if the bank agrees to allow the customer to overdraw in return for a consideration provided by him, the customer is legally entitled to overdraw on his account up to the agreed limit, and the bank will be liable to him in damages if it refuses to allow him to overdraw up to that limit, or if it dishonours cheques drawn by him within that limit.

It is uncertain whether a unilateral consent by a bank at a customer's request to allow an overdraft up to a certain limit creates a contract with the customer who expressly or impliedly accepts the facility. If there is a binding contract, it must be on the basis that the customer provides consideration for the bank's consent by expressly or impliedly promising to repay the overdraft plus interest and the bank's charges at the normal rates on demand. It is suggested, however, that there is no enforceable obligation on the bank to allow the customer to overdraw up to an agreed amount if the customer

---

[1] *Foley* v. *Hill* (1848) 2 H.L.C. 28.

merely promises to repay the amount actually overdrawn plus interest and charges. The reason for this is that the customer gives no consideration by making such a promise, because if the bank made advances to the customer equal to the overdraft facility without expressly agreeing to do so, the customer would be obliged to repay the advances actually made as debts incurred by him when the advances were made. The customer's promise to do this in return for the bank's promise to allow him to overdraw up to the agreed limit would therefore involve him doing no more than the law would require in any event. It would, of course, be otherwise if the customer agreed to pay interest on the amount of the overdraft facility whether he availed himself of the full facility or not, but the facility would then become a loan facility and would no longer be one for an overdraft.

If no contract arises when the bank agrees to give an overdraft facility, the bank may withdraw the facility by giving its customer notice to that effect. Nevertheless, if before it does so, the customer incurs an obligation to a third person in reliance on the facility (*e.g.* by issuing a cheque), the bank will incur liability to its customer if it does not discharge that obligation in exactly the same way as though the customer's account were sufficiently in credit. This is because, by its unilateral consent to the customer overdrawing up to a certain amount, the bank has induced him to act in a way which would result in him suffering a detriment if the consent were withdrawn (*i.e.* he will be liable on the obligation he has incurred to the third person). The bank is therefore estopped from denying that the customer was entitled as against the bank to draw up to the specified overdraft limit.[2] In this situation the fact that there was no actual contract between the bank and its customer becomes immaterial, and so does the fact that the customer gave no consideration for the overdraft facility.

(1) *Repayable on demand*

An overdraft is repayable by the customer immediately upon a demand being made on him by the bank, unless the bank has otherwise agreed. The banking practice of treating bank customers as obliged to repay overdrafts on demand in the absence of different terms is accepted as being the law. Loans or advances made by a bank when no date is agreed upon for repayment are, on the other hand, treated in law as implying a term that the loan or advance shall become repayable only when the bank has given the borrower a reasonable length of notice calling for repayment.[3]

There is only one judicial decision that a bank must give its cus-

---

[2] *Fleming* v. *Bank of New Zealand* [1900] A.C. 577.

[3] *Bradford Old Bank Ltd.* v. *Sutcliffe* [1918] 2 K.B. 833; *Buckingham & Co.* v. *London and Midland Bank Ltd.* (1895) 12 T.L.R. 70).

tomer a reasonable length of notice calling for repayment of an overdraft before issuing a writ to recover the amount owing by him.[4] The preponderance of judicial opinion is that a bank may demand immediate repayment of an overdraft at any time it thinks fit, and it owes no duty to the customer to ensure that the demand is made in sufficient time before it becomes effective so that the customer will have a reasonable opportunity to raise the money elsewhere if he does not have it in hand. On the other hand, the bank cannot treat the customer as being in default until it has given him sufficient time to obtain the money to repay the overdraft from a bank in the locality of his residence or business address, on the assumption that he has funds with such a bank. In other words, the customer is not in default until he has had time after the demand for repayment is made to fetch the money from a bank; it is no excuse on his part that there is no bank at which he has the money.[5]

There is one situation where a bank can recover the whole or part of an overdraft without first calling on its customer to repay it. This is where the bank has an immediate right to set off an item credited to the overdrawn account or to another account held by the same customer against the amount which he owes on the overdraft.[6] In this situation the bank does not seek to enforce its claim as a creditor against the customer, and so no preliminary demand is called for nor any notification of the bank's intention to exercise its right of set-off. If the customer is adjudged bankrupt, or being a company, goes into liquidation, statute directs that the mutual indebtedness of the customer and the bank to each other arising from the customer having two or more accounts, one or more of which are in credit and one or more of which are overdrawn, shall be set off and the balance only claimed by or from the bank.[7] The statutory insolvency rule is mandatory, and the parties cannot contract out of it.[8] Moreover, the rule applies, whether the amounts to be set off are immediately due or not, and so set-off of an overdraft must be effected against any credit balance in favour of a customer even though the bank has agreed to allow the customer time to repay it.

(2) *Limitation period*

Another problem arising from the rule that an overdraft is repayable on demand relates to the commencement of the statutory limi-

---

[4] *Brighty* v. *Norton* (1862) 3 B. & S. 305.
[5] *Toms* v. *Wilson* (1863) 4 B. & S. 442, 453 *per* Cockburn C.J.; *Moore* v. *Shelley* (1883) 8 App.Cas. 285, 293; *Cripps (Pharmaceuticals) Ltd.* v. *Wickenden* [1973] 1 W.L.R. 944; *Bank of Baroda* v. *Panessar* [1986] 3 All E.R. 751; [1987] 2 W.L.R. 208.
[6] *Garnett* v. *M'Kewan* (1872) L.R. 8 Ex. 10.
[7] Insolvency Act 1986, s.323(1), (2) and (4); Insolvency Rules 1986, r. 4.90(1), (2) and (4).
[8] *National Westminster Bank Ltd.* v. *Halesowen Presswork and Assemblies Ltd.* [1972] A.C. 785.

tation period within which the bank must sue its customer to recover the amount overdrawn on his account. The classical rule is that where a fixed sum is payable on demand under a contract or instrument which so provides expressly or by implication, the limitation period begins to run from the time when the obligation to pay is incurred, and not from the time when a demand for payment is made.[9] Consequently, it was held that an action to recover the amount of a promissory note which was expressed to be payable on demand was statute-barred six years after the note was issued, where no part payment or acknowledgment of indebtedness had been made by the promissor meanwhile, and this was so even though no demand for payment of the note had ever been made.[10] The courts have since held, however, that this rule does not apply when the plaintiff sues or relies on a collateral obligation, that is, if he seeks to enforce an obligation or a liability other than the indebtedness of the defendant. For this reason, as well as the fact that the debt was expressed to be payable on demand, Upjohn J. held in *Lloyds Bank Ltd.* v. *Margolis*[11] that a mortgage of land was not extinguished under the Limitation Act 1939, by 12 years passing from the date when the mortgage was executed, where the mortgage debt was expressed to be payable on demand and a demand for payment had only recently been made.

In all probability the reasoning in *Norton* v. *Ellam* is now obsolete. It is certain that a customer of a bank can recover the credit balance on his current account within six years after demanding payment, and the fact that his account has been dormant for more than six years since he last drew on it does not mean that the bank's obligation to pay is extinguished.[12] Parallel reasoning would lead to the conclusion that a customer's liability to repay an overdraft is not extinguished until six years after the bank demands payment. Unfortunately, however, there is a Court of Appeal decision that this is not so if an overdraft arises simply by a bank honouring cheques drawn by its customer whose account is insufficiently in credit to meet them.[13] The limitation period in that situation runs from the time when the bank actually demands repayment only if the customer has expressly contracted with the bank to repay advances made by it together with interest and charges "on demand."[14] The distinction between the two situations where the customer can be sued only in debt, because he has given no express promise to repay, or alternatively, where he can be sued for breach of contract because he has made an express promise to repay "on demand," is a slight

---

[9] *Norton* v. *Ellam* (1837) 2 M. & W. 461.
[10] *Ibid.*
[11] [1954] 1 All E.R. 734.
[12] *Joachimson* v. *Swiss Bank Corp.* [1921] 3 K.B. 110.
[13] *Parr's Banking Co. Ltd.* v. *Yates* [1898] 2 Q.B. 460.
[14] *Bradford Old Bank Ltd.* v. *Sutcliffe* [1918] 2 K.B. 833.

one, especially since the amount recoverable is the same in both cases, but the present state of the case law shows that the distinction is material.

(3) Disadvantages of overdraft financing

The great disadvantage of the overdraft as a means of financing companies' operations is that repayment may be called for without the bank giving any length of notice, and payment may therefore be demanded by the bank at a time when the company's liquid resources are low, even though its trading prospects are good and it is certain to have adequate resources to repay the overdraft in the fairly near future.

Efforts have been made in a number of recent cases where banks have taken steps to enforce securities taken by them for either overdrafts or term loans, to imply a duty on the part of the bank not to enforce its security when it is unreasonable to do so, that is, when the debtor company is financially sound, even though it may have committed a technical default.[15] All such attempts have failed so far. The court has held that the bank as a creditor owes no duty to its customer, the debtor, to act reasonably when deciding whether to take proceedings to recover a debt or to enforce a security for it, and the bank may consult only its own interests in deciding if and when to do so, and need not consider the interests of its customer. A creditor's duty of care arises only when he takes steps to enforce a security for his debt; he must then act reasonably to obtain the best available price, but the choice whether and when to enforce it is entirely his.[16] It follows that a bank may with impunity call in and enforce security given in respect of an overdraft at any time, and need not have regard to the effect of doing so on its customer. The customer may, of course, seek an extension of time to pay as a matter of grace, though not of right. If the bank concedes, even gratuitously, that it will give the customer an opportunity to raise funds elsewhere in order to discharge an overdraft, it cannot then call for immediate payment without giving the customer a reasonable opportunity to borrow elsewhere, or without at least giving the customer reasonable notice of the bank's intention to withdraw the concession.[17] On the other hand, although banks usually act fairly and considerately when there is a reasonable prospect of the customer surviving commercially, neither the law nor common sense requires them to defer calling for immediate payment of the amount owed on an overdraft, or enforcing securities for the overdraft, when there is no certainty that payment will be made. Certainty in this context is manifested only by a tender of payment.

[15] *Shamji* v. *Johnson Matthey Bankers Ltd.* [1986] B.C.L.C. 278.
[16] *Standard Chartered Bank Ltd.* v. *Walker* [1982] 1 W.L.R. 1410.
[17] *Williams and Glyn's Bank Ltd.* v. *Barnes* [1981] Com.L.R. 205.

7

Interest on overdrafts

Interest is calculated on overdrafts at the agreed rate or, if there is no agreement, at the bank's currently published lending rate. This is fixed by reference to the individual bank's minimum lending rate (which tends to be uniform for all the major commercial banks) plus a number of percentage points over the minimum depending on the creditworthiness of the customer. There is, of course, no reason why a bank and a customer should not agree specifically on the rate of interest to be charged, and the larger corporate customers of banks, who are in a stronger bargaining position than smaller customers, do bargain for and often obtain agreed lower rates of interest than those which the bank normally charges.

Overdraft interest is charged daily to the customer's account at the current rate on the debit balance at the close of business on the preceding business day. Consequently, in calculating overdraft interest, account is not taken of amounts credited to the customer's current account with the bank until the following business day, and if an overdraft is not reduced, the customer is charged with interest on a greater amount than is in fact outstanding on the day for which interest is charged. Conversely, of course, interest is not charged on amounts debited to the overdrawn account until the business day following that on which the drawing or transfer of funds, which gives rise to the debit, takes place. Overdraft interest is charged at quarterly or half-yearly intervals in accordance with the bank's practice, unless some other interval has been expressly agreed upon. If the interest for the quarter or half-year is not paid to the bank by the customer immediately, it is added to the amount of the overdraft on which interest is charged for the next and succeeding periods. Interest on a continuously overdrawn account can be a substantial component of the debit balance of the account at any time, and depending on the frequency of the interval at which overdraft interest is debited, the actual rate of interest charged over a year can be higher than the bank's current nominal annual overdraft rate. Nevertheless, unless the bank has led its customer to believe that interest would be charged in some other way, the bank is entitled in law to charge interest in this way in accordance with its normal practice.[18]

One advantage which an overdraft facility has over a loan of a fixed amount is that the customer pays interest only on the amount which he has overdrawn, and not on the as yet unused part of the overdraft facility, whereas interest may be charged on the whole amount of a loan of a fixed amount from the time it is made, even for a period when the customer has not drawn it down and the amount of the loan is merely credited to a loan account in the customer's

---

[18] *Gwyn* v. *Godby* (1812) 4 Taunt. 346; *Spencer* v. *Wakefield* (1887) 4 T.L.R. 194.

name. In practice, this advantage of an overdraft is illusory, because banks either credit undrawn amounts in loan accounts with periodic interest as though they were deposits with the bank, or, more usually, charge no interest on the undrawn part of a fixed loan, but instead charge a commitment fee at a low percentage rate on the part for the time being undrawn.

The other advantage of an overdraft facility is that the customer can repay the whole or part of the debit balance on his account at any time without giving the bank advance notice of his intention to do so, and by doing this he can immediately terminate interest charges if he repays the whole debit balance, or reduce the amount of interest charges in the future if he repays only part. If, on the other hand, a bank makes a term loan of a fixed amount, it is not obliged to accept repayment before the agreed repayment date or dates, or to accept partial repayments of principal. In practice, however, term loan agreements do permit the borrower to make advance repayments of the whole or part of the principal, but usually the borrower is empowered to do this only if he gives an agreed length of notice of his intention to repay, and each repayment must be a certain minimum figure or a multiple of that figure.

Purposes for which overdraft is used

The purposes for which a company borrows from a bank, whether by way of overdraft or by a fixed term loan, are not the concern of the law, provided the company has the necessary power to borrow expressed in the objects clause of its memorandum of association, or such a power is implied because the company was formed to carry on a business activity.[19] Even if the company has no such express or implied power to borrow, the bank may recover any advance it makes to the company, unless the bank actually knew that the company lacked the power to borrow or was exceeding the limits set by its memorandum of association on the amount it could raise by borrowing.[20]

If the company has power to borrow by the objects clause of its memorandum of association, but the bank is aware that its directors intend to use amounts which the bank advances to it for a purpose which is unrelated to the business which the company was formed to carry on, or that they intend to use advances for their own or a third party's benefit and not for the benefit of the company, the bank cannot recover the amount it advances to the company, whether by way of overdraft or fixed term loan, because the bank is then conscious that it is aiding the directors in committing a breach of their duties to the company.[21] However, if the bank is unaware of the use that

---

[19] *General Auction Estate and Monetary Co.* v. *Smith* [1891] 3 Ch. 432.
[20] Companies Act 1985, s.35.
[21] *Rolled Steel Products (Holdings) Ltd.* v. *British Steel Corp.* [1986] Ch. 246, C.A.

the directors of the company intend to make of advances made by the bank, or if the bank is unaware that the intended use is not for the purpose of carrying on the company's legitimate business, the bank's rights to recover the loan and to enforce any security for its repayment are unaffected, and can be enforced in the normal manner.[22]

Although the purpose for which a company borrows by way of overdraft may not be material when considering the legality of the borrowing, it will be of distinct importance in planning the financing of the company's activities and foreseeing the potential liability of its directors if it is eventually wound up in an insolvent condition. Originally banks financed companies by overdraft only so that they might carry on current trading transactions which would themselves provide the means for repaying or at least reducing the overdraft (*e.g.* the financing of purchases of raw materials by a manufacturing company, or the purchase of stock in trade by a wholesale or retail company). During the last 30 years however, the banks have increasingly financed the acquisition of capital assets by overdraft facilities. Such assets may be plant and machinery or existing businesses which the company adds to its original business. Acquisitions of capital assets certainly do not carry any assurance that the company will as a result earn sufficient profits to be able to discharge its short-term liabilities (including its indebtedness on overdraft) within the immediately forseeable future.

If overdraft financing is employed to enable a company to acquire capital assets, but the company is in the course of raising a long-term loan with which it will discharge the overdraft, no harm will be done to the company's solvency if the long-term loan is assured, and the overdraft will then serve the same purpose as a short-term bridging loan. Where, however, a company finances its expansion by using overdraft facilities, and it is neither large enough nor sufficiently sound to be certain of raising long-term share or loan capital when it needs it, the company courts the risk of becoming unable to pay its debts as they fall due. The likelihood of that happening will provide a strong inducement to its bank to demand immediate repayment of the company's overdraft, so making the winding up of the company inevitable. Directors of a company who finance its activities in this way by excessive short-term borrowing to meet capital expenditure, may additionally incur the risk of disqualification from holding any directorships in any company and also the risk of being compelled personally to satisfy the whole or part of the company's indebtedness in its liquidation, under the relevant statutory provisions.[23]

---

[22] *Re David Payne & Co. Ltd.* [1904] 2 Ch. 608.
[23] Company Directors Disqualification Act 1986, ss.4, 6, 10 and 11 and the Insolvency Act 1986, ss.213 and 214.

2. TERM LOANS

Term loans are made by banks to smaller companies for periods of up to five years (depending on the financial condition of the company and the use or uses to which the loan is to be put), and to larger companies and to particularly sound smaller companies for longer periods of up to 10 years or more. Term loans are always made at rates of interest which vary with current market rates during the life of the loan, and the agreement for a term loan always contains a provision for the acceleration of the repayment date if any of several specified contingencies occur. Some of these contingencies relate to defaults or breaches of contract on the part of the borrowing company, and others are concerned with changes in its financial condition or the state of its business undertaking. Very large term loans made to leading national and multinational companies are often made by a syndicate of banks. They share between themselves in agreed proportions the cost of providing the funds advanced to he borrowing company, and they are represented by one of their number, the lead bank, in negotiations and dealings with the company.

The advance and repayment of the loan

Term loan agreements usually provide that the borrowing company shall be given a facility by the lending bank or banks to borrow up to a stated amount (the maximum amount of the loan) and that the borrowing company may draw that amount down on stated dates during an initial period after the loan agreement is signed, either by a single drawing of the whole amount or by successive instalments none of which shall be less than a stated figure or a multiple of it. Amounts of the facility which have not been drawn by the end of the initial period may not be drawn thereafter, and the facility is then cancelled in respect of them. In the case of very large loans (particularly syndicated loans) the borrowing company is required to give a specified number of days' notice to the lending or lead bank that it intends to draw down a stated amount of the loan on the next drawing date. This is particularly important where the borrowing company has an option under the loan agreement to draw the loan down in any of several specified currencies, when the lending bank or banks will require advance notice so that they may obtain the required amount of the chosen currency by the drawing date. As already mentioned, banks always charge a small percentage fee (a commitment fee) on the undrawn balance of the maximum amount which they have agreed to lend to the borrowing company. This fee is charged periodically at the time when interest payments fall due, and it terminates when the whole amount which the bank has, or the syndicated banks have, agreed to advance has been drawn, or if the borrowing company does not draw the full amount, when the period during which drawings may be made comes to an end or the company notifies the bank or the lead bank that it does not intend to draw the balance of the loan facility.

Term loan agreements always specify the date or dates and manner by which the amount advanced by the lending bank or banks is to be repaid. In the absence of such a provision, the loan would be repayable on the bank or banks giving the borrowing company a reasonable length of notice demanding repayment,[24] but it would appear that the borrowing company would be entitled to repay such a loan at any time without giving any notice in advance of doing so. A term loan will by the loan agreement be repayable either in a single sum on one specified date, or more usually, by quarterly, half-yearly or (rarely) yearly instalments over a repayment period commencing on a date specified in the agreement. The commencement and duration of the repayment period are matters for negotiation between the borrowing company and the lending or lead bank, but subject to the overriding requirement that the lending bank or banks are not over-exposed to financial risk, the repayment period and the frequency of the repayment instalments are usually fixed by reference to the expected cash flow to the borrowing company from its business undertaking or from the assets or project which the loan is to finance.

The agreed repayment terms are reciprocally binding on the borrowing company and the lending bank or banks; consequently, the banks cannot require the company to repay the loan earlier than the date or dates agreed upon (unless the repayment date is accelerated under an applicable default clause), and the company, on its part, cannot save interest by repaying the loan before the agreed date or dates, although it may make an early repayment if it also pays interest in advance calculated up to the agreed repayment dates. It is usual, however, for term loan agreements to permit the borrowing company to repay the whole or part of the outstanding loan on any of the dates when interest is charged under the loan agreement, but again it is also usual to specify the earliest date on which this may be done, to require partial repayments to equal a stated minimum amount or multiples of that amount and to make it a condition of pre-payment that the borrowing company gives the lending bank or the lead bank a certain length of notice of its intention to repay the loan in whole or part.

Conversion into non-recourse loans

Term loans made to large companies to finance projects or developments which will be income-producing on or soon after com-

---

[24] *Buckingham & Co.* v. *London and Midland Bank Ltd.* (1895) 12 T.L.R. 70.

pletion (*e.g.* loans to finance the exploration for, and exploitation of, oil bearing localities, the construction and eventual sale and disposal of industrial complexes overseas) sometimes contain an option for the borrowing company to convert the outstanding balance of the loan on any date for repayment of an instalment during the repayment period into a non-recourse loan if certain specified financial conditions are fulfilled. The non-recourse loan always carries a higher rate of interest than the initial loan, but as its name implies, it is repayable with interest during a period longer than the initial repayment period out of the earnings or return of the project or development financed by the initial loan. Moreover, the loan and the higher rate of interest are repayable only out of those earnings, without any personal liability on the part of the borrowing company which could result in the company's insolvency and consequent liquidation. For example, the terms of a non-recourse loan into which an initial loan made to finance the exploration and development of an oil field is converted, may make the non-recourse loan repayable with interest by instalments out of the proceeds of sale of crude oil obtained and sold during successive quarterly or half-yearly periods following completion of the work for drilling the oil wells in that field, and the amount of each instalment will be calculated by reference to the proportion between the oil so produced during the quarter or half-year and the proved or estimated reserves of the oil field.

The value of a non-recourse loan facility to the borrowing company is that the company is no longer personally liable to repay the outstanding loan, which is now charged exclusively on the project which the loan was used to finance, and the lending bank or banks cannot resort to the company's other assets if the loan is not fully repaid. Those other assets are therefore available for the company to sell, lease or otherwise dispose of free from any charge or security created under the loan agreement, and they are also available to be used as security for further borrowing by the company.

On the other hand, the lending bank or banks do not take an equity participation in the project or development which the initial loan is used to finance. The bank or banks are still creditors of the borrowing company, and they may recover out of the future earnings or returns of that now completed project or development the whole outstanding balance of the loan with interest on it at the agreed higher rate, insofar as those future earnings or returns are sufficient for the purpose. Nevertheless, non-recourse loans are often made repayable by a specified future date at the latest, and if the earnings of the project or development do not suffice to discharge the outstanding principal and interest by that date, the lending bank or banks are given power by the loan agreement to appoint a receiver to take over the future management of the project or development or to sell the company's assets comprised in it. If additionally the com-

13

pany is to be responsible for payment of any part of the loan and interest thereon which has not been received by the lending bank or banks by the specified date, the non-recourse loan reverts to being a normal loan on that date, and the company's personal liability and the bank or banks' normal remedies for enforcing it revive.

Interest

Interest on term loans made by banks is invariably charged at a rate which varies with the market rates during the currency of the loan, so that the lending bank or banks may borrow for comparatively short terms (usually quarterly or half-yearly) on the market in order to provide for the continuance of the loan during the period for which it was made. In other words, the risk of interest rates rising during the loan period is borne entirely by the borrowing company, and the lending bank or banks are assured of receiving a fixed margin of interest over the current market rate throughout the loan period. This contrasts with the traditional arrangement when a public company raises a long-term loan by issuing debenture or loan stock to the public. Under such an issue the rate of interest payable to the debenture or loan stock holders is the same throughout the loan period, and is fixed by reference to the market rate of interest prevailing when the loan is raised. The risk of changes in interest rates during the loan period is therefore borne by the lenders, and if interest rates rise, the market value of their debenture or loan stock inevitably falls.

(1) *Interest formulas*

The formula for fixing periodic interest rates under a term loan is usually that the borrowing company is empowered to select the interest period which is to apply, whether monthly, quarterly or half-yearly, but rarely a longer period. On a specified date preceding the commencement of each such period there is to be taken an objective rate of interest (such as the lending bank's base rate on that date, or the London Inter-Bank Offered Rate (LIBOR) for three month deposits in sterling on that date, or in the case of Euro-dollar loans the current offered rate of interest for three month deposits of US dollars with banks in New York), and there is to be added to that objective rate an agreed number of percentage points (the bank's margin). The contractual rate of interest on the term loan during the ensuing interest period is then the sum of the objective rate so ascertained and the agreed margin. On very large loans the contractual interest rate is sometimes fixed by taking as the objective rate (to which a margin is added) the average of the daily LIBOR or Euro-dollar offered rate during the three months or six months preceding the commencement of the interest period, and sometimes also such a rate is fixed, not prospectively, but retrospectively at the end of an interest period by reference to the average daily objective rate during that period. If for any reason the objective rate of interest cannot be ascertained on the relevant date, or if it is the current offered rate for sterling or Euro-dollar deposits and the lending bank or banks cannot obtain deposits at that rate, there is usually incorporated in the loan agreement an arrangement by which a substituted interest rate to be charged for the ensuing interest period may be ascertained. Also in syndicated loan agreements it is usual to provide that any lending bank may withdraw from the loan and require repayment of any amount it has already advanced, if it cannot obtain deposits at the objective rate of interest.

Term loan agreements normally provide that interest shall be paid by the borrowing company at the agreed rate at the end of each interest period, but where the term loan is made to finance a project or development which will not produce earnings or a return for a protracted time, it is common to provide that interest payments falling due in the early part of the loan period may at the option of the borrowing company be capitalised and added to the principal of the loan. Interest will then be charged on that capitalised sum in future interest periods, and the capitalised interest will be repayable in addition to the principal of the loan during the repayment period defined by the agreement by the instalments specified in it.

(2) Penal interest

Prompt payment of interest where there is no option for the borrowing company to capitalise it is normally ensured in one of four ways. The first is by the loan agreement charging a higher or penalty rate of interest for the interest period and during the time an interest payment is delayed. This is of questionable validity. From the 17th century onwards equity has treated the imposition of a higher rate of interest than the contractual one if an interest payment is made late as being a penalty against which equity would give relief, and the borrower can therefore discharge his obligation to pay interest by paying it at the contractual rate calculated up to the date of actual payment.[25] On the other hand, equity permits the same result to be achieved by the converse method, namely by the lender charging a higher contractual rate of interest in the loan agreement, but agreeing that it shall be reduced to the rate the lender really requires if prompt payment is made. Equity construes this as entitling the borrower to pay the lower rate of interest only if the condition for prompt payment is strictly complied with, and if late payment is made the lender can charge the higher rate of interest.[26] Foreign systems of law, particularly those of the Western European countries,

---

[25] *Holles* v. *Vyse* (1693) 2 Vern. 289; *Hunter* v. *Seton* (1802) 7 Ves. 265.
[26] *Wallingford* v. *Mutual Society* (1880) 5 App.Cas. 685; *Maclaine* v. *Gatty* [1921] 1 A.C. 376.

do not treat provisions for penal rates of interest or other penalties for the failure to fulfil contractual obligations with the same condemnation as English law, but regard them as the contractual price the defaulting party agrees to pay for his default. Since the validity of a penalty provision is a matter of substantive law to be governed by the proper law of the contract and not the *lex fori*, it would seem therefore, that in international loan agreements where either the lending bank or the borrowing company is governed by a non-British system of law, it may well be that a provision for penal rates of interest when there is a default in making an interest payment will be valid and enforceable.

Despite the invalidity of penal rates of interest under the English rules of equity, it has been held that a provision in a loan agreement was valid by which commission would be charged at a monthly percentage rate calculated on the principal of the loan for any delay in making interest payments.[27] The reason for this decision would appear to be that the charge of commission did not increase the interest payable for the interest period, but was a separate contractual payment which could only be invalidated in equity if it bore no relationship to the economic loss suffered by the lender as the result of the delay in the payment of interest. If this is so, it would appear that equity would treat as valid a provision for a reasonable increase in the contractual rate of interest on an interest payment which is made late if the increased rate is not charged for the interest period itself, but only for the delay in its payment, that is, for the period between the date when the interest payment should have been paid and the later date on which it is actually made. Such a provision would seem to be subject to invalidation only if the interest for the period of delay will be charged at a rate greatly in excess of the contractual rate and therefore disproportionate to the loss of income which the lender has suffered because of the delay.

(3) *Default interest*

The second way in which the prompt payment of interest may be ensured or, at least, the delayed payment of interest may be made expensive, is by the loan agreement providing that interest at a higher rate than the contractual rate shall be charged on the amount of an interest payment which is not paid on the due date. This is really a variant of the third form of constraint for prompt payment, namely, compounding interest which is in arrear by automatically, or at the option of the lending bank, adding unpaid interest to the principal of the loan so that interest at the contractual rate is charged on it for all subsequent interest periods. The difference from a compounding provision is, of course, that the borrower can stop

---

[27] *General Credit and Discount Co.* v. *Glegg* (1883) 22 Ch.D. 549.

interest at the higher rate accruing on the delayed interest payment by making that payment plus accrued interest on it at the higher rate at any time, whereas under a true compounding provision the interest payment which is overdue becomes part of the principal of the loan and interest is charged on it for the whole remainder of the loan period.

(4) *Compounding*

A provision by which unpaid interest is automatically compounded, or is compounded if it is in arrear for more than a specified number of days, is valid if clearly drafted, but any ambiguity in the compounding provision will be construed against the interests of the lender and may make it ineffective.[28] Likewise, an option for the lending bank to compound unpaid interest is valid if clearly expressed and the exercise of the option is notified to the borrowing company. Nevertheless, it should be remembered that the compounding of interest, whether automatically or by the exercise of an option, converts the unpaid interest into principal for all purposes. Consequently, the lending bank is not able to treat the borrowing company's failure to pay interest which has been compounded as a default entitling the bank to exercise the appropriate remedies available if a borrower defaults, unless the bank's right to do so is expressly reserved. In this respect a provision for the payment of default interest at a higher rate than the contractual rate on an interest payment which is delayed is preferable to compounding, because the lender can recover the interest payment plus default interest at any time as a debt which is immediately due, and can also treat the non-payment of interest as an event of default entitling the lender to accelerate the date for repayment of the loan.

(5) *Acceleration provisions*

The final provision in a loan agreement which is designed to ensure the prompt payment of interest is the one already mentioned, namely, one which accelerates the contractual date for the repayment of the principal of the loan if an interest payment is not made on the due date or within a specified number of days thereafter. Such a provision is usually part of a larger one dealing with the lending bank's powers and remedies on the borrowing company's default in any respect under the loan agreement, and so it will be considered later in this Chapter in that connection. It is only necessary to note here that an acceleration provision is not regarded as a penalty by equity, and so is valid and effective if properly drafted.[29] This is so even if the acceleration provision is combined with one for the charging of default interest or for the compounding of unpaid interest.

---

[28] *Ferguson* v. *Fyffe* (1841) 8 Cl. & Fin. 121; *London Chartered Bank of Australia* v. *White* (1879) 4 App.Cas. 413.
[29] *Keene* v. *Biscoe* (1878) 8 Ch.D. 201; *Wallingford* v. *Mutual Society* (*supra*).

17

Warranties and representations

It has become the practice in recent years for loan agreements entered into by banks to contain a number of warranties or representations about the financial and legal position of the borrowing company and the validity and effectiveness of the loan and the terms of the loan agreement. This has come about by the adoption in this country of the practice of American banks, and it is employed particularly where the loan is a foreign currency loan or is made to an overseas company.

Often the borrowing company in the loan agreement both makes representations and gives warranties about the specified matters, but sometimes it makes only representations. The distinction between the two in the present context is technical rather than of substantial significance. A warranty is a contractual undertaking which forms part of the loan agreement, and its distinguishing feature is that it relates to the existence of a state of affairs (*e.g.* the present indebtedness of the company), and not to something which the company undertakes to do or to procure to be done in the future. The remedy for a breach of warranty is an action by the lending bank or banks for damages for breach of contract.

A representation is not part of the loan agreement, but an inducement given by the borrowing company to the lending bank or banks to enter into that agreement. The basic remedy in equity for the lending bank or banks if the representation turns out to be false or unfounded, is to rescind the loan agreement. This entails the immediate repayment of the amount advanced to the borrowing company. By statute, however, the lending bank or banks may alternatively or additionally claim damages from the company for any loss they have suffered as a result of the representation proving false, and the company can escape liability for damages only if it can prove that it had reasonable grounds for believing that the representation was true at the time it was made.[30]

In practice banks do not pursue the remedies made available by law for breaches of warranties or the non-fulfilment of representations in loan agreements. Instead they rely on the provision invariably inserted in the agreement that any breach of warranty or misrepresentation on the part of the borrowing company shall be an event of default. This will entitle the lending banks or banks to exercise the remedies given by the loan agreement and by law to recover immediately the amount advanced to the company, plus interest, fees, costs and charges, and if the loan is secured or guaranteed, to realise the security created for the loan or to enforce the guarantees. The reason for the bank choosing to treat the breach of warranty or the misrepresentation as an event of default is obvious. If the bank

---

[30] Misrepresentation Act 1967, s.2(1).

18

relied on the remedies given by law, it would at most have an unsecured claim in debt or for damages against the borrowing company. If it treats the breach of warranty or the misrepresentation as a default under the terms of the loan agreement, it can accelerate the repayment date of the loan and recover immediately the amount payable to it on the company's default in accordance with the loan agreement, either by suing the company, or by realising any security for the loan or enforcing any guarantees.

Usual warranties and representations

The warranties or representations which are included in a loan agreement usually comprise the following commitments:

(i) that the borrowing company is duly incorporated under the laws of the country where it is registered, that it has power to enter into the loan agreement on the terms it contains and that the agreement has been duly authorised by the appropriate organs of the company;

(ii) that the company has taken no corporate action and no action has been taken against it, as a result of which it may be wound up, dissolved or re-organised, or a receiver, trustee or similar officer may be appointed in respect of it or its assets or revenues;

(iii) that the borrowing company has not defaulted under any agreement to borrow (or, often, under any agreement of any kind) which it has entered into and which is currently operative, and no event has occurred as a result of which the company may commit such a default in the future;

(iv) that the audited accounts of the company for its most recent complete financial year fairly represent its financial condition, and that since the date to which those accounts were made up, there has been no material adverse change in the financial condition of the company;

(v) that the information given to the lending bank or banks in the course of negotiations for the loan (whether comprised in an information memorandum submitted to the banks or otherwise) was and still is true, complete and accurate in all material respects;

(vi) that no incumbrance or charge over any of the assets or revenues of the company exists, and no litigation which may have a material effect on the company's business, assets or financial condition has been commenced or is threatened, otherwise than as disclosed by the company before the signing of the loan agreement.

The warranties or representations provide the basis on which the loan is made, and if the loan agreement provides a loan facility by which a maximum sum may be drawn down by instalments, it is important that the warranties or representations should be effective at the date when each instalment is drawn. This is achieved by the so-called "evergreen" clause inserted in the loan agreement, by which the warranties or representations are deemed to be repeated on each occasion a drawing is requested by the borrowing company. Consequently, under such a clause if any warranty or representation has ceased to be true since the loan agreement was entered into, the company commits a default when it requests a further drawing, and the lending bank or banks may act accordingly.

Borrowing company's covenants

Loan agreements entered into by banks always contain lengthy covenants by the borrowing company designed to ensure that it will conduct its business properly, and that it will not engage in activities which may put its solvency at risk or jeopardise any security which has been given for the amounts payable to the lending bank or banks. These covenants are contractual undertakings by the company to do or to abstain from doing specified acts during the continuance of the loan agreement, and the remedies given by law for breach of any of the company's covenants are an action for damages to compensate the lending bank or banks for any consequential loss suffered by them, or if the breach is fundamental, the termination of the loan agreement and the immediate recovery of the amount advanced and interest, fees and costs remaining unpaid.

Again, however, the practical significance of the covenants to the lending bank or banks lies not in the remedy of an action for damages against the borrowing company or in the possibility of terminating the loan agreement for fundamental breach, but in the fact that the loan agreement will expressly make a breach of any of the borrowing company's covenants an event of default. The occurrence of any event of default will by the terms of the loan agreement entitle the lending bank or banks to exercise the remedies given by the agreement to recover the amount of principal, interest, fees, costs and charges payable to it or them immediately, to realise any security created by the loan agreement and to enforce any guarantees given under it. The covenants serve not so much as promises the non-fulfilment of which give rise to unsecured claims in debt or for damages against the borrowing company, but as conditions any breach of which entitles the lending bank or banks to exercise the remedies given by the loan agreement in order to recover immediately the whole amount which is owing under it to them.

(1) *Usual covenants by the borrowing company*

The borrowing company's covenants are always expressed to continue in force as long as any amount payable under the loan agreement remains unpaid. The principal covenants by the borrowing company found in most loan agreements include the following:

(i) to pay all amounts which fall due under the terms of the loan agreement, whether instalments of principal, interest, fees, charges or other sums, immediately upon them falling due;

(ii) to conduct and carry on the borrowing company's business in a proper and efficient manner, and not to make any substantial change in the nature or mode of conducting its business without the consent of the lending bank;

(iii) to apply the amounts borrowed under the loan agreement only for the purpose of conducting the borrowing company's business or acquiring fixed and other assets to enable it to do so, or if the purpose of the loans is more specifically defined by the loan agreement, not to apply the amounts borrowed under it for any purpose other than that specified purpose;

(iv) to keep all buildings, plant, machinery, fixtures, vehicles and office and other equipment of the company in good condition; to insure all the company's insurable assets for their full replacement value; to fulfil and conform with all covenants and other obligations of the company under leases or hiring agreements entered into by it in respect of land, buildings, plant or equipment leased or hired to the company; to fulfil all obligations of the company under licences to use or exploit patents, trade marks and other industrial property rights held by it; and not without the consent of the lending or lead bank to vary, cancel, assign or charge any such lease, hiring agreement or licence;

(v) to furnish copies of the company's audited annual accounts and unaudited quarterly or half-yearly accounts or financial statements to the lending bank or banks; to notify the bank or banks of the occurrence of any event of default under the loan agreement; and to furnish the bank or banks annually and on demand with a certificate by two or more senior officials of the company that no event of default and no act or event which may result in an event of default has occurred;

(vi) to ensure that the company's working capital (*i.e.* current assets less current liabilities) is maintained at not less than a specified sum, that its tangible net worth (*i.e.* paid up share capital and capital and revenue reserves less goodwill and taxation and revaluation reserves) does not fall below a specified figure, that the ratios between the company's tangible net worth and total liabilities and between its current assets and current liabilities do not fall below specified minima, and that dividends and other distributions made by the company to its shareholders (including redemptions and purchases of shares) do not exceed a specified percentage of the company's

21

net profits for the year in respect of which the distribution is made or its cumulative net undistributed profits;

(vii) not to create any mortgage, charge or incumbrance on the whole or any part of the assets of the company without the prior written consent of the bank, subject to any relaxation of this restriction for financing current transactions which is written into the covenant.

(2) *Restrictive effect of covenants*

The practical problem in drafting and negotiating the covenants which are entered into by the borrowing company is to maintain a balance between the need of the lending bank or banks to ensure that the company maintains its business in a solvent condition, and does not impair its ability to make all payments which are due or may become due to the bank or banks, yet at the same time to leave sufficient management freedom to the company's directors so that they may carry on the company's business profitably and may exploit business opportunities without constantly having to seek the banks' permission before engaging in normal current transactions. The greater elaboration of companies' covenants in recent years has created the danger of restricting management freedom and enterprise too severely, and in practice technical breaches of companies' covenants in loan agreements often occur without the lending banks treating the matter as an event of default, or even being made aware that the events have occurred. The remedy for this would seem to lie in a more careful drafting of the provisions of the loan agreement which identify the events of default, and the confinement of the rash of covenants which often decorate banks' standard forms of loan agreements to those which are really important.

Events of default

The last and probably the most important provision in a bank loan agreement is the one which lists the various events which will cause the borrowing company to be in default, and which will then entitle the lending bank or banks to exercise the remedies given by the loan agreement or by law, in order to realise any security for the loan and to enforce any guarantees which have been given in respect of it. It has become the practice in recent years for the list of events of default to be kept fairly short, and for the list to concentrate on events which create or may create a serious risk that the company will not be able to repay the loan and other amounts owing to the lending bank.

Default clauses are always drafted so as to give an option to the lending bank to declare the company in default so as to avoid a default occurring automatically on the occurrence of an event of default. Where there is an ambiguity in a default clause, the courts incline toward construing it as merely giving the lending bank such an option, and not as putting the company in default automatically.[31] Even if a default provision is expressly made automatic in operation, it is always possible for the lending bank to waive it on the occurrence of a particular default, without prejudicing its right to invoke the provision on a subsequent occasion because of the occurrence of the same or a different kind of default.[32] The danger in relying on the lending bank's power to waive defaults is that, because the default has in fact occurred, the company may be in default under other agreements it has entered into in consequence of cross-default provisions contained in them, and the other parties to those lending agreements may not be willing to give waivers. This can, of course, have an adverse effect on the bank under whose agreement with the company the original default occurs, because for practical reasons it finds that it cannot risk waiving the default if its own interests are to be safeguarded. However, what are often referred to as waivers of a default are often not waivers at all; if the default clause is properly drafted so as to give the lending bank the right to declare the company in default, a decision by the lending bank not to exercise its option to treat the company as being in default is not a waiver, but the prevention of a default occurring at all.

Usual events of default

The events which bank loan agreements always make the principal events of default so as to enable the lending bank to demand immediate payment by the borrowing company, are as follows:

(i) the failure by the company to pay any amount owing under the loan agreement on the due date for payment;

(ii) the failure by the company to fulfil any of the covenants entered into by it in the loan agreement, or to comply with any provision of the agreement;

(iii) any warranty or representation made or repeated by the company in or in connection with the loan agreement, or any statement, certificate, account or information furnished by the company under the loan agreement being incorrect or incomplete at the time it is made, repeated or furnished;

(iv) an order being made or a resolution being passed for the winding up or dissolution of the company or for the administration of its assets, or the suspension of payments by the company or the appointment of a receiver of the whole or a substantial part of the company's assets or business undertaking;

---

[31] *Governments Stock and Other Securities Investment Co.* v. *Manila Ry. Co.* [1897] A.C. 81.
[32] *Panoutsos* v. *Raymond Hadley Corp. of New York* [1917] 2 K.B. 473.

(v) the company proposing or entering into an agreement with its creditors for a composition, moratorium or arrangement in respect of its debts and liabilities, whether approved by the court or not;

(vi) any distress, execution or attachment being levied on any assets of the company;

(vii) the company ceasing or threatening to cease to carry on all or a substantial part of its business undertaking;

(viii) an amount borrowed by the company becoming due before its normal date for payment as a result of the occurrence of any event under any other loan agreement entered into by the company (the so-called "cross default clause").

With the extension by recent legislation of the impact on individual creditors of the initiation of insolvency proceedings against a company, it has become common in recent years to counteract the statutory invalidation of action taken by lending banks in their own interests if they leave it too late before intervening, by anticipating defaults by borrowing companies and making events which indicate that defaults may occur into events of default themselves. Thus, bank loan agreements now often make any of the following an event of default, namely, the presentation or threatened presentation of a petition for the winding up of the borrowing company, or the presentation or intended presentation of a petition for the making of an administration order in respect of the company, or the calling of a meeting of shareholders to pass a resolution for the voluntary winding up of the company. The obvious purpose of such provisions is to give the lending bank or banks an option to intervene and to realise its or their security as soon as there is a threat or a possibility of insolvency proceedings, and so forestall any possibility of the borrowing company's assets being made available to its creditors generally.

The latest elaboration of this tendency is the recent practice of some banks to include in their standard forms of loan agreement a residual provision that it shall be an event of default "if any other event or series of events occurs which in the opinion of the bank may affect the ability or willingness of the company to comply with all or any of its obligations under this agreement." Although the inclusion of such a provision may be justifiable, because a lending bank cannot foresee all possible changes in the circumstances of the borrowing company, it must be accepted that the use of such a provision narrows considerably the distinction between a term loan and a loan which is repayable on demand, and leaves the company at the mercy of a subjective judgment by the bank that there is a risk that it may default, not that it has done so.

II

Bank Finance for Specific Purposes

The first Chapter of this book examined the ways in which banks make loans to companies or provide advances for them in order to finance their activities in general. Overdraft facilities are inevitably of this general character, and often term loans are as well. It is true that term loans made to finance particular projects or developments are usually made on condition that the loan shall be used for no other purpose, and the loan is then often secured on the assets of the project or development. But these are merely contractual additions to a loan agreement which would be similar in structure if the loan were made for the company's general purposes, and even if a loan is made to finance a specific project, it may still be secured on the company's assets and undertaking as a whole.

Quite distinct from such financing of companies for agreed purposes are the different kinds of transactions which are entered into by banks, or more usually, their specialised subsidiaries, in order to provide companies with the finance, or the assurance of the availability of finance, which they need in connection with certain classes of business dealings. These specific kinds of bank financing transactions range from the issue of letters of credit by banks in connection with import and export sales to the sale of trade debts owed to companies by their customers in return for the immediate payment of the discounted present value of such debts to the companies by banks or their subsidiaries. The forms of financing transactions by which banks provide the money needed by companies for current or capital purposes have grown immensely in variety and complexity over the last 15 years, and transactions which would have formerly have been considered outside the field of banking activities have now become everyday and commonplace. The transactions are specialised, however, and because they call for talents different from those of the traditional banker, most of the commercial banks and some of the merchant banks have formed or acquired separate subsidiary companies to engage in them. This is, of course, merely a matter of policy or practice, and not an invariable rule, and particular banks may retain some of these new forms of business themselves, notwithstanding the tendency toward establishing specialised subsidiaries. For example, some banks issue letters of credit to finance the international sale of goods through their overseas departments, whereas letters of credit and guarantees in connection with the acquisition of business undertakings and investment transactions abroad are issued by their subsidiaries which specialise in capital investment or in investment management or new issue activities. From a legal point of view these administrative arrangements are immaterial. It is the form and character of the transaction and the role played in it by the bank or its subsidiary which is important.

1. LETTERS OF CREDIT

Financing of export and import transactions

The original and still today the commonest purpose for which banks issue commercial letters of credit is to finance import and export transactions in goods. Whether the goods in question are supplied by a British exporter to an overseas buyer or by an overseas seller to a British importer, the seller requires an assurance beyond the personal commitment of the buyer to pay the price plus incidental transportation and insurance costs as a safeguard against the buyer's possible insolvency. The bank commercial credit supplies this assurance, and if the credit is issued by a British or overseas bank of sound reputation, the credit is as valuable in the seller's hands as an equivalent credit to his own bank account.

The form of a bank commercial credit is nowadays either a cash or deferred payment credit by which the bank undertakes to pay the amount due from its customer, the buyer, to the seller, on or at an agreed time after the presentation of specified shipping documents, showing that the goods in question have been despatched to the buyer, or alternatively, an acceptance credit by which the issuing bank undertakes on the presentation of the requisite shipping documents to accept a bill of exchange drawn on it by the seller payable at a specified future date.

A variant of the acceptance credit is the negotiation credit, by which the issuing bank agrees to purchase at its face value a bill of exchange drawn by the seller on the buyer for the amount payable to the seller under the contract of sale. On presentation of the shipping documents, the bank either credits that amount to an account for the benefit of the seller on which the seller may draw when the bill of exchange falls due for payment, or the bank makes an immediate payment to the seller of the discounted value of the bill of exchange, that is, its face value less interest at the current market rate for the period up to the date when the bill matures. A seller may similarly obtain an immediate cash payment under an acceptance credit after the acceptance of the bill drawn under it by the issuing bank; he may do this by selling the bill either to the issuing bank or to his own bank for the discounted face value of the bill.

An additional complication may be introduced by the contract between the seller and the buyer requiring the commercial credit issued by the buyer's bank to be confirmed by a second bank in the seller's country, or in the country in whose currency payment under the credit is to be made. The second or confirming bank then adds its undertaking to that already given by the issuing bank in exactly the same terms, and if the credit calls for the acceptance or negotiation of a bill of exchange by the banks, it is usually the confirming bank which will give the acceptance (if required) or which will discount the bill, although there is nothing to prevent the seller presenting the bill drawn under the credit direct to the issuing bank.

Basic legal features of bank commercial credits

The detailed law relating to bank commercial credits is outside the scope of this book, but two of its features should be noted in passing. The first of these is that the issuing and confirming banks are legally bound to take up the shipping documents tendered by the seller and to accept or negotiate the bill of exchange tendered with the shipping documents only if those documents comply exactly with the requirements of the letter of credit. This is often difficult to achieve, because the shipping documents (*i.e.* a bill of lading, air waybill, road or rail consignment note plus an insurance policy or certificate for the goods in transit) are prepared by persons other than the seller (shipping line, airline, railway or road transport undertaking or an insurance company) and the seller has no direct control over the way in which those persons frame the documents. Nevertheless, the burden of exact compliance is imposed on the seller as a condition which must be fulfilled if the issuing and confirming banks are to be called on to pay the amount for which the letter of credit is issued, or to accept or negotiate a bill of exchange for that amount. Even disparities between the terms of the letter of credit and the documents tendered which are commercially insignificant or which are accepted as normal in commercial practice, will entitle the issuing and confirming banks to reject the shipping documents and to refuse to honour the credit.[1] The other cardinal feature of the law governing commercial credits is that the issuing or confirming bank is concerned only to ensure that the shipping documents tendered to it are formally in order, and it is neither obliged nor entitled to require the seller to prove that the statements of fact in those documents are correct (*e.g.* weight, quantity or condition of the goods consigned).[2] The House of Lords has even held that if the tendered shipping documents comply formally with the conditions of the letter of credit, the issuing or confirming bank can refuse to take them up and to honour its obligations under the credit only if it

---

[1] *Donald H. Scott & Co. Ltd.* v. *Barclays Bank Ltd.* [1923] 2 K.B. 1; *J. H. Rayner & Co. Ltd.* v. *Hambro's Bank Ltd.* [1943] 1 K.B. 37.

[2] *Hamzeh Malas* v. *British Imex Industries Ltd.* [1958] 2 Q.B. 127; *Basse and Selve* v. *Bank of Australasia* (1904) 20 T.L.R. 431.

can prove that the seller has been guilty of fraud, and the fact that one or more of the shipping documents are forgeries or that they have been falsified by third persons without the concurrence of the seller does not entitle the bank to reject them.[3] The correctness of this decision is very doubtful, and the decision of the Court of Appeal, which the House of Lords overruled, that an issuing or confirming bank need not accept shipping documents which are forgeries or which have been falsified, whether the seller is responsible for or connived at the forgery or falsification or not, would seem preferable and in line with the previous decisions of the Court of Appeal and the courts of first instance.[4] It would seem very odd indeed that an issuing or confirming bank should be obliged to take up shipping documents which to its knowledge are forgeries and worthless and do not represent goods conforming to the terms of the credit, and that it should be obliged to pay or to commit itself to pay the amount of the credit in return. Letters of credit are not negotiable instruments, but even if they were, a *bona fide* purchaser for value of a forged or falsified document issued under them would not be able to enforce the obligation embodied in them as a holder in due course, because forgery or falsification of the documents would destroy its negotiable quality.

Letters of credit as financing vehicles

The issue or confirmation of a bank commercial credit may operate to finance either the buyer or the seller or both in connection with an international sale transaction. If the buyer does not put the issuing bank in funds to meet its obligations under the credit before it issues it, the bank incurs an immediate obligation to the seller upon issuing the credit, and it will have to satisfy that obligation by paying the amount of the credit to the seller or accepting or negotiating a bill for that amount whether or not it has meanwhile been put in funds by the buyer. The issuing bank therefore provides the buyer with a financial facility by issuing the credit, and if it has not been paid an equivalent amount by the buyer beforehand, it will make an advance to him when it pays the seller under the credit or when it pays a bill of exchange accepted or negotiated by it under the credit. If the commercial credit is confirmed by a second bank, that bank does not provide any further financial facility for the buyer, and there is no legal relationship between it and the buyer.[5] The confirming bank enters into an obligation to the seller to honour the credit, but as between itself and the issuing bank and the buyer it

---

[3] *United City Merchants (Investments) Ltd.* v. *Royal Bank of Canada* [1983] 1 A.C. 168.
[4] [1981] 1 Lloyd's Rep. 604; *Kwei Tek Chao* v. *British Traders and Shippers Ltd.* [1954] 2 Q.B. 459; *Etablissements Esefka International Anstalt* v. *Central Bank of Nigeria* [1979] 1 Lloyds Rep. 455.
[5] *Calico Printers Association* v. *Barclays Bank Ltd.* (1930) 36 Com.Cas. 71.

acts as an agent for the issuing bank. Consequently, it must look to the issuing bank for the reimbursement of amounts paid by it under the credit, and it is entitled to reimbursement only if it can deliver to the issuing bank shipping documents which conform exactly to the conditions specified in the letter of credit.[6]

An issuing bank and a confirming bank obviously provide a financial facility for the seller by means of a letter of credit which is issued to him, because they thereby incur an obligation to make a payment to him in the future if certain conditions are fulfilled. The seller's contractual rights to payment or the acceptance or negotiation of a bill of exchange under a letter of credit may be assigned by him to a third person in the same way as he may assign other contractual rights by a legal or equitable assignment, and he may also create an equitable charge over his rights under a letter of credit by an agreement which shows that he intends to make them available as security for a debt which he owes to a third person. However, the seller cannot transfer the right to draw bills of exchange under a credit, unless the letter of credit expressly so provides, because in the absence of such a provision the letter of credit will oblige the issuing and confirming banks only to accept or negotiate a bill of exchange for the amount of the credit which is drawn by the beneficiary named in the credit, namely, the seller and no-one else. This has been held to be so under the general law by an American court,[7] and is undoubtedly so under English law too. Consequently, if the seller wishes to enable the assignee or chargee of his rights to payment under the credit to enforce them against the issuing and confirming banks, the seller must himself sign as drawer all bills of exchange which are to be presented under the credit, unless the letter of credit expressly permits him to transfer this right too.

Although a bank commercial credit provides a financial facility for the seller, payments made under it by the issuing or confirming banks are obviously not made by way of an advance, but in discharge of the buyer's obligation to pay the price and other incidental amounts under the contract of sale which occasioned the issue of the credit. Because of this, an issuing or confirming bank which negotiates a bill of exchange drawn on the buyer under a negotiation credit cannot recover the amount it pays to the seller by exercising its normal right of recourse as indorsee of the bill and suing him as drawer and payee of it if the bank is not reimbursed by the buyer as drawee.[8] It is true that the issuing or confirming bank takes the bill of exchange as an indorsee from the seller, who is the payee, and under the rules governing the liability of parties to a bill of exchange the bank would be entitled to recover the amount of the bill from the

---

[6] *Bank Melli Iran* v. *Barclay's Bank D.C.O. Ltd.* [1951] 2 Lloyds Rep. 367.

[7] *Erikkson* v. *Refiners Export Co.* (1942) 35 N.Y.S. 2d 827.

[8] *M. A. Sassoon & Sons Ltd.* v. *International Banking Corp.* [1927] A.C. 711.

seller as a prior indorser if the drawee, the buyer, does not pay it. However, the liability of the bank to the seller as the beneficiary of the letter of credit overrides the bank's right of recourse under the bill of exchange, and it impliedly waives any right of recourse when it negotiates the bill.

Although an advance is not made by the issuing or confirming bank to the seller when the bank honours its obligations under a letter of credit, it is possible for the seller to use the credit as a means of raising finance (*e.g.* for the purpose of acquiring or manufacturing the goods he has agreed to supply to the buyer). The seller may do this either by assigning or charging his rights under the letter of credit in the way indicated above, or if the credit is an acceptance credit, by the seller discounting the bill of exchange for cash after its acceptance by the issuing or confirming bank. By these means the seller may obtain an immediate payment of the discounted value of the bill of exchange which has been or will be drawn under the credit.

The issuing bank's right to reimbursement

The person who is principally financed by the issue of a bank commercial credit is, of course, the buyer, unless he pays the issuing bank the amount for which it makes itself liable to the seller at the time when the letter of credit is issued, or unless he authorises the issuing bank to transfer that amount immediately from the credit balance of an account he has with it. It is in practice rare for a bank to issue a letter of credit at the request of its customer without requiring him to sign written instructions detailing the terms and conditions on which the credit is to be issued, and providing also for the eventual reimbursement of the bank by the customer and for the payment by him of the bank's expenses and charges for its services. Nevertheless, it is important to ascertain the rights and security which the issuing bank would have in the absence of express written instructions signed by the customer. These rights and security are available to the bank in any event if not excluded by the express terms of its customer's instructions, and it is therefore often necessary to discover whether and to what extent the instructions add to the bank's rights under the general law.

(1) *Conditions for claiming reimbursement*

An issuing bank is entitled to claim reimbursement from its customer for amounts paid by it under a bank commercial credit issued at his request plus the bank's expenses and charges. The bank may claim reimbursement either under the contract arising from the bank's acceptance of the customer's instructions, or as money paid for the use of the customer at his request. Nevertheless, the issuing bank is entitled to reimbursement only if the instructions of the customer have been complied with exactly; if the bank or any of its agents (including a confirming bank) has failed to do so, the bank loses its right to reimbursement, and moreover is liable in damages to its customer for its breach of contract.[9] Exact compliance means the same in the context of a claim by the issuing bank for reimbursement as it does in the context of a claim to have the credit honoured made by the beneficiary of a commercial credit who has tendered the documents called for by the credit to the issuing or confirming bank.

However, it has long been held that if an issuing or confirming bank takes up shipping documents in good faith from the beneficiary, and they comply formally with the conditions of the customer's instructions to the issuing bank but include forged or falsified documents, the issuing bank is still entitled to reimbursement by its customer.[10] The one exception to this is that the issuing bank cannot claim reimbursement if it accepts or negotiates a forged bill of exchange which has been drawn by an unauthorised third person and not by the beneficiary of the credit, and the same would appear to be the case if the bill of exchange has been altered without the beneficiary's authority.[11] The reason for this exception is that the issuing bank's mandate from its customer is limited to accepting or negotiating a bill of exchange drawn by a named person, the beneficiary, and even if the issuing or the confirming bank acts in good faith in accepting or negotiating a forged bill, the issuing bank acts outside it mandate, and consequently forfeits its right to reimbursement. This reasoning does not apply if any of the shipping documents taken up by the issuing or confirming bank are forged or falsified, because the bank's obligation in respect of such documents is to take them up if they are formally in order and on a reasonable inspection appear to be genuine.[12]

(2) *The bank's right to advance indemnification*

An issuing bank which makes payment to the beneficiary of a letter of credit is clearly entitled to reimbursement when it has acted in accordance with its customer's instructions. It is also entitled to advance indemnification by its customer and to be put in funds to make the payment a reasonable time before the payment becomes due under the terms of the letter of credit or a bill of exchange

[9] *Equitable Trust Co. of New York* v. *Dawson Partners Ltd.* (1926) 25 Lloyds L.R. 90; *South African Reserve Bank* v. *Samuel & Co. Ltd.* (1931) 40 Lloyds L.R. 291; *Borthwick* v. *Bank of New Zealand* (1900) 6 Com.Cas. 1.

[10] *Woods* v. *Thiedemann* (1862) 1 H. & C. 478; *Gian Singh & Co. Ltd.* v. *Banque de l'Indochine* [1974] 2 Lloyds Rep. 1.

[11] *Orr* v. *Union Bank of Scotland* (1854) 1 Macq.H.L.Cas. 512; *British Linen Co.* v. *Caledonian Insurance Co.* (1861) 4 Macq.H.L.Cas. 107; *Slingsby* v. *District Bank Ltd.* [1932] 1 K.B. 544).

[12] *United City Merchants (Investments) Ltd.* v. *Royal Bank of Canada* [1983] 1 A.C. 168.

accepted under it.[13] If the customer does not put the issuing bank in funds before payment to the beneficiary becomes due, the bank may either pay the amount due and recover it from its customer with interest at its current lending rate, or it may borrow in order to pay the amount due and recover from its customer the amount borrowed plus the rate of interest paid to the lender if it is a reasonable commercial rate.[14] However, if the issuing bank becomes insolvent or goes into liquidation, or if a receiver is appointed of its assets and undertaking, before the customer is obliged to put it in funds to make payment to the beneficiary, the customer's obligation is terminated, because he now has no assurance that the bank will pay the beneficiary on the due date.[15] To require the customer to put the issuing bank in funds in these circumstances would expose him to a double liability; if, as is likely, the bank does not pay the amount due to the beneficiary on the maturity date, the customer would remain liable to pay the beneficiary personally under the contract between them.

Furthermore, it would appear that if the customer in fact puts the bank in funds either before or after it becomes insolvent or goes into liquidation or receivership, the bank holds the funds on trust to fulfil the purpose for which they were paid to it, namely, to pay the beneficiary, and this trust can be enforced against the bank or its liquidator or receiver by the beneficiary or by its customer.[16] Alternatively, the customer may reclaim the amount paid as money paid for a consideration which has wholly failed, but it would then rank simply as an unsecured creditor of the bank.

(3) Security for reimbursement

An issuing bank has not only a personal claim against its customer for reimbursement of the amount paid by it to the beneficiary of a letter of credit issued on the customer's instructions plus its expenses and charges, but is also entitled to security for its claim to which it may resort to obtain reimbursement. When the bank accepts or negotiates a bill of exchange under the letter of credit, or if the credit is a cash or deferred payment credit, when the bank pays the beneficiary, the bank acquires an equitable charge over the goods represented by the shipping documents which it takes up as well as a common law lien over the documents themselves.[17] Whether the bank's equitable charge over the goods arises under an

---

[13] *Reynolds* v. *Doyle* (1840) 1 M. & G. 753; *Yates* v. *Hoppe* (1850) 9 C.B. 541.

[14] *Re Ludwig Tillman* (1918) 34 T.L.R. 322.

[15] *Sale Continuation Ltd.* v. *Austin Taylor & Co. Ltd.* [1968] 2 Q.B. 849.

[16] *Re Kayford Ltd.* [1975] 1 W.L.R. 279; *Carreras Rothman Ltd.* v. *Freeman Matthews Treasure Ltd.* [1985] Ch. 207.

[17] *Re Barned's Banking Co., Coupland's Claim* (1869) 5 Ch.App. 167; *Guaranty Trust Co. of New York* v. *Hannay & Co.* [1918] 2 K.B. 623; *Midland Bank Ltd.* v. *Eastcheap Dried Fruit Co. Ltd.* [1962] 1 Lloyds Rep. 359.

implied term in the contact between the bank and its customer, or whether it is an equitable lien arising by operation of law, is immaterial in practice, because the rights of the bank are the same in both cases, but they can be varied or supplemented by the terms of the instructions taken by the bank from its customer for the issue of the credit.

When imported or exported goods arrive at their destination, it is usual for the buyer's bank to release the shipping documents relating to them to the buyer so that he may collect them and either resell them or use them for the purpose of his own business. The bank's equitable charge or lien over the goods continues notwithstanding the release of the documents to the buyer, and the bank may recall the goods, or enforce its charge by selling the goods, if the buyer does not pay the amount he owes the bank on demand or in accordance with such other terms as have been agreed.[18] However, the possession of the shipping documents by the buyer with the bank's consent gives him an apparent authority to sell the goods represented by them, and a purchaser who acquires the goods in good faith from the buyer without notice of the bank's charge or of any limitation on the buyer's authority to dispose of them, obtains a title to the goods free from the equitable charge in favour of the bank, as does a second bank which makes an advance on the security of the goods in like circumstances.[19]

(4) Trust letters and receipts and letters of hypothecation

The release by the buyer's bank of goods or the shipping documents relating to them when the buyer has not reimbursed the bank is usually effected on the terms of a trust letter or receipt signed by the buyer acknowledging that he holds the goods and the proceeds of any sale of them by him as an agent or trustee for the bank. Often the terms of a trust letter or receipt are incorporated in the written instructions which the buyer gives to the bank to issue the letter of credit. Alternatively, the buyer delivers to the bank a letter of hypothecation or charge by which he charges the goods and the proceeds of selling them with payment of the amount owing by him to the bank; or, more probably, he will have delivered to the bank a general letter of hypothecation or charge by which he gives an anticipatory charge over all goods which he purchases with the aid of finance provided by the bank, and the anticipatory charge attaches in equity to particular goods as and when he acquires them by means of letters of credit issued by the bank or advances made by it.[20]

[18] *Sewell* v. *Burdick* (1884) 10 App.Cas. 74.

[19] *Merchant Banking Co. of London* v. *Pheonix Bessemer Steel Co. Ltd.* (1877) 5 Ch.D. 205; *Union Bank of Canada* v. *Cole* (1877) 47 L.J.C.P. 100; *Babcock* v. *Lawson* (1879) 4 Q.B.D. 394; *Commonwealth Trust Ltd.* v. *Akotey* [1926] A.C. 72.

[20] *Holroyd* v. *Marshall* (1862) 10 H.L.C. 191; *Re Bond Worth Ltd.* [1980] Ch. 228.

The effect of trust letters or receipts and letters of hypothecation or charge is exactly the same, namely, they create an equitable charge in favour of the bank over the goods and the proceeds of sale.[21] This contractual charge is of the same quality as the equitable charge or lien which arises by implication when shipping documents are released by the bank to the buyer so that he may collect and dispose of them. Consequently, the rights of the bank and any purchaser of the goods from the buyer are the same, whether the bank simply releases the shipping documents to the buyer, or whether it has him sign a trust letter or receipt or a letter of hypothecation or charge as well. The only danger from a purchaser's point of view is that if he takes delivery from the buyer, not of the goods, but of the shipping documents relating to them, and in disposing of the shipping documents the buyer is acting in breach of the terms of the trust letter or receipt he has signed, the bank can sue the purchaser for conversion of the shipping documents at common law, and the purchaser's good faith is then no defence.[22]

Other uses of bank letters of credit

The financing of the import and export of goods is not the only purpose for which letters of credit issued by banks may be used. They are extensively employed in the United States to facilitate and to finance the sale and purchase of investments and business undertakings, although they are not yet much used for these purposes in the United Kingdom, where the security usually required by a seller who is uncertain of the buyer's ability to pay the price is either a substantial deposit or a guarantee of the purchase price given by a bank or both. Letters of credit are also sometimes used in the United Kingdom, as they are in the United States, as a means of creating a short or medium term loan facility either for a customer of the bank which issues the credit, or for a third person with whom the customer has a business relationship, for example, a contract for the construction of a building or for engineering work. A direct contract is then created between the bank and the beneficiary, who is entitled to draw on the bank, and if by the terms of the credit it is the bank's customer, and not the beneficiary, who is to reimburse the bank and pay its commission and expenses, a contract is also created between the bank and its customer.[23] One result of such a direct contractual relationship between the bank and the beneficiary where the bank's customer is to reimburse the bank, is that when the beneficiary draws on the credit, the bank cannot set off against the amount to be paid to the beneficiary any amount which its customer owes to it.

[21] *Re Bond Worth Ltd. (supra)*.
[22] *Midland Bank Ltd.* v. *Eastcheap Dried Fruit Co. Ltd.* [1962] 1 Lloyds Rep. 359.
[23] *Re Agra and Masterman's Bank, Ex p. Asiatic Banking Corp.* (1867) 2 Ch.App. 391.

Letters of credit under which amounts may be drawn, but are not certain to be drawn, are usually known as facility or standby credits. If the credit is issued to the bank's customer, it provides machinery for activating a loan facility; if it is issued to a third person it may similarly enable a loan facility to be used, but more often in practice it serves as a guarantee of a payment which the bank's customer will or may have to make to the third person. Stand-by credits in favour of third persons are therefore best considered in connection with bank guarantees and performance bonds.

2. BANK GUARANTEES AND PERFORMANCE BONDS

Bank guarantees and performance bonds, which are a species of guarantee, are connected functionally with letters of credit, and the law in respect of both forms of bank financing has developed along similar lines. Neither a bank guarantee nor a performance bond provides finance directly for a bank customer, but by assuring the other party to a transaction entered into with the customer that the customer's obligations under the transaction will be fulfilled, the guarantee or bond enables the customer to acquire rights against the third party under the same transaction, and so the customer will acquire assets, services or a money payment from the third person according to the terms of the transaction.

Bank guarantees in lieu of letters of credit

Bank guarantees can be used instead of bank commercial credits to finance the import or export of goods, and this is often done. The only legal difference between a letter of credit and a bank guarantee in this context is that under a letter of credit the issuing bank is the primary debtor to whom the seller must resort before claiming the price and other amounts due under the contract of sale from the buyer.[24] Under a guarantee, on the other hand, the buyer is the primary debtor, and the bank is only secondarily liable to the seller.

However, the distinction is not of great practical importance, because the seller can sue the bank under the guarantee without first suing the buyer if he fails to pay the amount due to the seller,[25] and a bank which gives a guarantee will usually require the buyer to agree that the shipping documents shall be delivered to it, and not directly to the buyer, so that the bank may have an equitable lien or charge over them. Moreover, the terms of the bank guarantee usually provide in the seller's interest that the bank shall be deemed as between itself and the seller to be a principal debtor for the amount payable

---

[24] *Soproma S.p.A.* v. *Marine and Animal By-Products Corp.* [1966] 1 Lloyds Rep. 367; *Newman Industries Ltd.* v. *Indo-British Industries Ltd.* [1956] 2 Lloyds Rep. 219.
[25] *Walton* v. *Mascall* (1844) 13 M. & W. 452).

to the seller under the guaranteed contract of sale (not exceeding a stated sum). Such a provision prevents the bank from invoking defences under that contract, and from contending that it has been released from its guarantee by modifications of the terms of that contract subsequently agreed upon by the seller and the buyer without the bank's assent.

Other bank guarantees: guarantees callable on demand

Distinct species of bank guarantees have emerged in recent years in connection with international contracts for the supply or purchase of goods and contracts for construction projects or the provision of services. The supplier of goods or services or the contractor under a construction project may require a guarantee that a deposit will be paid when the contract with the bank's customer is entered into, or that the balance of the price and other amounts payable to the supplier will be paid when it has carried out its part of the contract. A purchaser of goods or services or an employer under a construction project may require an initial guarantee that the bank's customer will commit itself contractually when the customer submits a tender for a contract; or the purchaser or employer may require a guarantee that any deposit which the purchaser or employer pays to the customer will be returned if the customer's obligations under the contract are not fulfilled; or the purchaser or customer may require a guarantee that the bank's customer will perform its obligations under the contract fully, and will pay damages for breach of contract if it does not do so.

If such guarantees are expressed objectively, so that they impose liability on the guarantor bank only if the party whose performance it guarantees fails to fulfil its obligations to the other party, the bank is not liable under the guarantee unless the other party can prove that this has in fact happened. Moreover, if the guarantor bank makes a payment under the guarantee without ensuring that there has been such a default, it cannot recover an indemnity from its customer on whose behalf it gave the guarantee. However, international guarantees are often framed in the form of an undertaking by the bank to make payment on demand by the other party, or on the other party alleging that there has been a default. In that case the bank must make payment on demand, and cannot insist on proof that there has in fact been a default.[26] The bank's customer whose performance is guaranteed cannot obtain an injunction to prevent the other party calling on the bank for payment, or to prevent the bank making payment in response to such a call, and if the bank

---

[26] *Howe Richardson Scale Co. Ltd.* v. *Polimex-Cekip* [1978] 1 Lloyds Rep. 161; *Intraco Ltd.* v. *Notis Shipping Corp. (The Bhoja Trader)* [1981] 1 Lloyds Rep. 256.

makes payment despite its customer's instructions not to do so, the bank may nevertheless recover an indemnity from its customer.[27]

The only occasion when the customer may obtain an injunction to prevent the bank making payment under the guarantee is where the other party is joined as a party to the proceedings and it is proved, or a substantial case is made out, that the other party has been guilty of fraud, or that the contract with the other party has been terminated otherwise than by the unilateral act of the bank's customer.[28] The bank can, of course, rely on the fact that the guarantee it has given is itself void or voidable (e.g. for illegality, fundamental mistake or misrepresentation), or that the guarantee has expired or has been terminated (e.g. by the other party releasing the bank from liability under it). It would seem that if for either of these reasons the bank could resist the enforcement of the guarantee, it owes a duty to its customer whose performance is guaranteed to refuse payment, or at least to ascertain and act upon his wishes, and if the bank does not do so, it will be unable to claim an indemnity from him.[29]

In other respects performance bonds are governed by the general law relating to guarantees, and they are in fact merely a species of guarantee which has acquired a special name because of their prevalence in international transactions, and because the amount guaranteed is usually payable on demand without proof of default. Despite their name, performance bonds need not be in the form of deeds. A signed guarantee issued by a bank in return for valuable consideration is as effective as a bond under seal. Performance bonds have been compared to letters of credit in the decided cases, but only because of the feature they usually possess of being enforceable on the presentation of a claim that there has been a failure to perform the guaranteed act, in the same way as a bank commercial credit may be enforced on the presentation of the requisite documents without the need to prove that the subject matter of the credit (usually goods) exists and will be transferred to the bank's customer.

3. STERLING COMMERCIAL PAPER

During the 18th and 19th centuries the acceptance and discounting of bills of exchange as a means of providing short term finance for business undertakings was one of the main functions of the hundreds of banks which then existed, particularly the small private banking partnerships which carried on business in most of the main cities and towns of this country. With the growth of joint-stock banking in

---

[27] *R. D. Harbottle Mercantile Ltd.* v. *National Westminster Bank Ltd.* [1978] Q.B. 146; *Edward Owen Engineering Ltd.* v. *Barclays Bank International Ltd.* [1978] Q.B. 159.

[28] *Edward Owen Engineering Ltd.* v. *Barclays Bank International Ltd.* (*supra*); *Bolivinter Oil S.A.* v. *Chase Manhattan Bank N.A.* [1984] 1 W.L.R. 392.

[29] *Bolivinter Oil S.A.* v. *Chase Manhattan Bank N.A.* (*supra*).

the latter two-thirds of the 19th century, this function diminished in comparison with the more modern forms of bank financing, the overdraft and the short term loan, but often loans in those forms were still supported by promissory notes given by the borrowers and their guarantors. Bank financing through bills of exchange and promissory notes has never completely disappeared, however, and during the 1960's the bill of exchange and the acceptance credit were for a while extensively used again for the temporary financing of companies which had already borrowed extensively and consequently found it difficult to raise further loans from the banks or elsewhere.

The regulations relating to sterling commercial paper

In May 1986 the promissory note re-appeared in the form of sterling commercial paper as an alternative vehicle for the short term financing of companies. The date of the re-appearance of promissory notes in this form can be fixed with exactitude, because it was necessary for the Government to add to the exemptions from the licensing requirements of the Banking Act 1979, to make their issue lawful, and this was done by the Banking Act 1979 (Exempt Transactions) (Amendment) Regulations 1986.[30] By the Banking Act 1979, subject to certain exceptions, no person or company may accept deposits of money in the course of carrying on a deposit taking business, unless the Bank of England has authorised them to do so.[31] The issue by a company of promissory notes or of undertakings to repay money advanced to it for use in carrying on its business would therefore be an infringement of this prohibition, if the company issued such paper repeatedly and were not authorised to accept deposits, and so a special exemption from the Banking Act 1979, was required if a market in short term commercial paper issued by trading companies was to be created.

The 1986 Regulations authorise a company to issue sterling commercial paper in return for money advanced to it if the date for repayment is not earlier than seven days, nor more than one year, after the date of issue, but the authorisation is given only to companies which have a listing for their shares on the Stock Exchange of the United Kingdom and Ireland and to the wholly-owned subsidiaries of such listed companies which issue sterling commercial paper guaranteed by their parent company. A listed company which accepts the deposit or which guarantees sterling commercial paper issued by its wholly-owned subsidiary must according to its latest

---

[30] S.I. 1986/769. See now Banking Act 1979 (Exempt Transactions) Regulations 1986 (S.I. 1986/1712), para. 15.

[31] Banking Act 1979, s.1 and s.2(1) (now re-enacted by the Banking Act 1987, s.3(1) and (2)).

audited annual accounts have net assets of not less than £50 m.[32] Each note issued as sterling commercial paper must relate to a deposit of not less than £500,000 and must be transferable in units whose repayment value is not less than £500,000.[33] Finally, sterling commercial paper must not be guaranteed by any person other than a recognised bank or licensed deposit taker, or if the issuer is a wholly-owned subsidiary, by its listed parent company.[34] As regards it form, sterling commercial paper must confirm on its face that it has been issued in compliance with the 1986 Amendment Regulations (now para. 15 of the Banking Act 1979 (Exempt Transactions) Regulations 1986), and must state whether or not it is guaranteed by a recognised bank or licensed deposit taker and if so must name the guarantor. Moreover, unless it is issued under a prospectus or listing particulars governed by the Companies Act 1985 or the Financial Services Act 1986, sterling commercial paper must state that the issuing company or its listed parent company which guarantees payments under the paper, has fulfilled its obligations under the Stock Exchange Listing Regulations 1984 and the Financial Services Act 1986, and that there has been no significant adverse change in that company's ability to fulfil its obligations as they fall due since it last published information about itself under the 1984 Regulations and the Financial Services Act 1986.[35]

Status as promissory notes and negotiable instruments

Sterling commercial paper may take the form of a promissory note, but it will not necessarily do so. The advantages of it being a promissory note are that it can be made payable to a named person or order (and so be transferable by indorsement and delivery) or to bearer (and so be transferable by delivery alone), and furthermore, a holder who purchases it in good faith and for value will acquire a perfect title to it free from any defects in the title of previous holders.[36] Moreover, the holder of a lost or destroyed promissory note may require the issuer to provide a replacement, or may sue on the lost or destroyed bill on giving an appropriate indemnity to the issuer.[37] The fact that the sterling commercial paper contains the information required by the 1986 Regulations will not prevent it

---

[32] Banking Act 1979 (Exempt Transactions) (Amendment) Regulations 1986, para. 3, inserting a new para. 16 in the Banking Act 1979 (Exempt Transactions) Regulations 1983 (S.I. 1983/1865).

[33] *Ibid.*

[34] *Ibid.*

[35] Banking Act 1979 (Exempt Transactions) Regulations 1982, para. 16(1) (added by 1986 Regulations, para. 3) (now Banking Act 1979 (Exempt Transactions) Regulations 1986, para. 15(1)).

[36] Bills of Exchange Act 1882, ss.29, 31, 38, 83 and 89.

[37] *Ibid.* s.69.

from being a promissory note, because this in no way affects the promise it contains to pay a fixed amount of money on a future date.

Moreover, it has been held that sterling commercial paper may still be a promissory note despite the fact that it does not contain an express promise to pay, but merely an acknowledgment of the deposit of a certain sum with the issuer which the paper says will be repaid at a stated future date with or without interest.[38] The acknowledgment of the deposit would not be a promissory note, however, if it merely stated that the deposit is repayable on or after a certain date, because there is then no affirmation that it will be repaid on that date from which a promise to repay may be inferred.[39] Moreover, it has been held by the Court of Appeal in a recent decision that a document is not a promissory note unless it contains an express promise to pay a sum of money, and that it is not sufficient for it to imply a promise to do so.[40] Consequently, if this last decision is correct, documents which merely contain receipts for money or acknowledge the deposit of money will not be promissory notes, even if they specify the date on which the money will be repaid with our without interest.

In practice sterling commercial paper will either contain an express promise to pay a certain sum on a stated future date, and will be issued at a discounted lower price to take account of interest at the current market rate for the period from the issue of the note until its maturity, or the paper will acknowledge the deposit of a certain sum with the issuer, or the payment to the issuer of that sum, and will state that that sum will be repaid with interest at a specified rate calculated from the date of issue to the date of maturity. The first, but not the second, form of commercial paper will therefore be a promissory note. It must be remembered, however, that for the purpose of the 1986 Regulations the amount of the deposit in respect of which sterling commercial paper is issued will be the amount paid by the first holder to the issuing company, which if the paper does not carry interest, will be less than the amount payable to the holder on maturity. To comply with the Regulations, the amount of the deposit must not be less than £500,000.

There is nothing in the 1986 Regulations to prevent the nominal amount of sterling commercial paper being made repayable by instalments, and provided that all the instalments are repayable on fixed dates, the arrangement for repayment will not prevent the paper taking the form of a promissory note.[41] In practice a company which wishes to raise money to be repaid by instalments will issue two or more series of notes for parts of the total sum raised, and all

---

[38] *Casborne* v. *Dutton* (1727) 1 Selwyn's N.P. 329.
[39] *Akhbar Khan* v. *Attar Singh* [1936] 2 All E.R. 545.
[40] *Claydon* v. *Bradley* [1987] 1 W.L.R. 521.
[41] Bills of Exchange Act 1882, s.9(1) and s.89(1).

the notes in the same series will be repayable on the same date, the different series themselves being repayable on a succession of dates. There is nothing to prevent the terms of issue of sterling commercial paper providing for the accelerated payment of the paper if certain events occur, such as the issuing company going into liquidation or receivership. If this is done, however, the paper cannot qualify as a promissory note, because the dates when the accelerating events may occur and, indeed, the possibility that they may occur at all during the currency of the paper, will result in the maturity date of the paper not being certain when it is issued.[42]

It is uncertain whether sterling commercial paper which does not satisfy the conditions for promissory notes will be recognised by market practice as being negotiable so as to acquire the status of negotiable instruments at common law. Certificates of deposit issued by banks and other financial institutions since the 1970's are in the same position of uncertainty, although there is evidence that the market does treat them as negotiable if they are in bearer form. The advantage of negotiability would, of course, be that a holder in due course of sterling commercial paper would acquire a good title to it if he took it in good faith and for value, even though the person from whom he acquired it had no title or a defective title.

The market for sterling commercial paper

When the market for sterling commercial paper was initiated in May 1986, it was envisaged as providing an alternative facility for companies to raise short-term advances to finance their current trading, so reducing their reliance on bank advances. Also there was the cosmetic object in mind that since the amounts advanced on sterling commercial paper would not figure in the published aggregates of bank lending or the money supply, the substitution of sterling commercial paper for borrowing from the banks would help to slow down the rate of increase in those aggregates. The intention was that sterling commercial paper would be taken up or purchased by financial institutions other than banks (the discount houses, finance companies and some institutional investors) and also by companies holding surplus funds which they would otherwise invest in short term securities on the money market. It is, in fact, unlikely that the commercial banks or the merchant banks will invest in sterling commercial paper, but their specialised subsidiaries may well do so, and if the market in sterling commercial paper proves successful, the banks will thus indirectly participate in it. In any event, this new facility for the short-term financing of companies is so closely related to the other financial facilities which the banks already pro-

---

[42] *Crouch* v. *Credit Foncier of England Ltd.* (1873) L.R. 8 Q.B. 374; *Bechuanaland Exploration Co.* v. *London Trading Bank* [1898] 2 Q.B. 658.

vide that it deserves consideration in a survey of bank finance for companies.

4. FACTORING

Factoring agreements

There has been a remarkable increase in the last 20 years in the provision of short and medium term finance for companies engaged in the manufacture and distribution of goods and in the provision of services by means of the purchase for cash by specialised companies of trade debts payable to the supplying companies by their customers. Trade debts are represented by the invoices which the companies send their customers when the goods are supplied or services rendered, but as invoices usually provide that one or more months' credit is allowed to the customers, a supplying company therefore has a continuous immediate need for short term funds to meet its own current operating costs until the invoices are paid. If a company is engaged in manufacturing or supplying capital goods or carrying out medium term projects overseas, the period between the incurring of expense by the company and the settlement of accounts by its customers is often much longer than one or two months, and the company's need for immediate cash payment in order to balance its outgoings is then even more acute.

The business carried on by the specialised companies which have been formed to acquire other companies' trade debts in return for immediate cash payments is known as factoring in the United Kingdom and forfaiting in European countries. Many factoring companies have been acquired by the commercial banks and operate as their subsidiaries, and some commercial banks have formed new subsidiaries to establish a presence in the business of factoring. The term "factoring" is derived from the business carried on during the 18th and 19th centuries by commodity brokers and intermediaries in the marketing of manufactured goods who bought, sold and stored goods on behalf of their principals in the United Kingdom and overseas in return for a commission. These brokers and intermediaries often made advances to their principals on the security of the goods they held on the principal's behalf, and it is from this financial aspect of traditional factoring that the modern expression is derived. Modern factoring companies do not in fact handle goods physically, but confine themselves to financing the marketing of goods and services, although some factoring companies are connected to shipping lines, airlines and forwarding agents who do handle, store and transport goods.

A typical modern factoring agreement contains an undertaking by the manufacturing or distributing company to offer the whole or a certain portion of its trade debts represented by copies of invoices sent to its customers for purchase by the factor, and in return the factor agrees to acquire the whole or a revolving maximum amount of those debts, provided that they satisfy certain conditions as to credit, creditworthiness of the customers, etc., so as to assure the factor that the debts will be paid. The purchase price paid for the debts by the factor is their discounted value (after deducting interest at an agreed rate from their nominal value) less a commission and the factor's charges for collecting the debts. Usually a percentage of the net amount after these deductions is retained by the factor, and is paid to the company only when the acquired debts have been paid, or after an agreed interval.

If the manufacturing or supplying company collects the trade debts itself after they have been purchased by the factor (as it sometimes contracts to do as the factor's agent), the factoring agreement provides that the company will hold the proceeds in trust for the factor, and will account for them to the factor forthwith or at intervals. Usually, however, the factor also provides the service of collecting the trade debts itself and keeping the necessary accounting records, in which case the invoices sent out by the manufacturing or supplying company will instruct its customers to pay the factor direct, but they do not necessarily disclose the factoring arrangements agreed between the company and the factor.

If the factor is unable to collect debts which it has acquired because customers do not pay, the company may be required to make good the deficiency under the terms of the factoring agreement, which is then known as a recourse factoring agreement. On the other hand, the factor more usually agrees to accept the risk of bad debts itself in return for a higher rate of commission or increased charges to the company whose debts it acquires, and by the terms of such a non-recourse factoring arrangement the factor is either not compensated at all for the amount of the acquired debts it cannot recover, or it may be permitted to compensate itself only by resorting to the percentage of the discounted value of the debts which it retains out of the price it pays for them to the company.

Legal questions in connection with factoring

A factor under a modern factoring agreement is an assignee of the debts it acquires from the manufacturing or supplying company. It acquires these debts as a purchaser in consideration of the agreed price which it pays to the company; even if it reserves a right of recourse against the company when any of the assigned debts is not paid, it remains a purchaser of the debts with the benefit of a guarantee, and is not treated as a mortgagee of the debts for an advance on the security of them to the company.[43] If a factor does in fact

---

[43] *Re George Inglefield Ltd.* [1933] Ch. 1; *Lloyds and Scottish Finance Ltd.* v. *Prentice* (1977) 121 Sol.Jo. 847.

make an advance to the company on the security of an express charge over its trade debts, the transaction will, of course, be treated as a mortgage or charge, and the court's interpretation of it will not be influenced by the fact that normally the factor purchases the company's book debts.[44] One of the consequences of a factor taking a charge over book debts from a company instead of purchasing them is that the charge will have to be registered at the Companies Registry in order to preserve its validity in the liquidation of the company and against other secured creditors who also have charges on the debts.[45] A factoring agreement in the normal form is not a mortgage, and so does not require registration.

The assignment of trade debts under a factoring agreement will be a legal assignment if three conditions are fulfilled, namely, the debts exist when the assignment is made (although they need not be due at that time), the assignment is in writing signed on behalf of the assigning company and is absolute in terms (which it may be despite a contractual obligation of the company to re-purchase the debts if the factor cannot recover them), and notice in writing of the assignment is given to the debtors.[46] The advantages of a legal assignment are that the factor, as assignee, can sue the debtors to recover the amounts they owe without the assistance of the company, and can give the debts a good discharge for their debts without the concurrence of the company.

In practice assignments under factoring agreements are usually equitable in character for a variety of reasons. In the first place, the factoring agreement will relate to trade debts owing to the assigning company both at the time of the agreement and in the future after the agreement is entered into; the intended assignments will take effect in equity immediately the debts come into existence, but there will be a legal assignment only if the company executes a separate written assignment to the factor after the debts arise.[47] Secondly, it is unusual for the company or the factor to give express notice of the assignment of a trade debt to the debtor before it becomes due, and if when it becomes due the debt is paid to the factor or to the company in trust for the factor, the debtor is discharged and there is no occasion for giving notice to him. Nevertheless, the company will usually instruct its customers to pay trade debts which they owe to it direct to the factor, without disclosing the reason for this instruction, and the instruction is usually embodied in the invoices sent to the customers. Such an instruction is itself an equitable assignment of the debt to which it relates, and also a notice of that assignment to the debtor so that he can only obtain a discharge for his indebted-

---

[44] *Independent Automatic Sales Ltd.* v. *Knowles and Foster* [1962] 1 W.L.R. 974.

[45] Companies Act 1985, s.395(1) and s.396(1)(e).

[46] Law of Property Act 1925, s.136(1).

[47] *Tailby* v. *Official Receiver* (1888) 13 App.Cas. 523; *Siebe Gorman & Co. Ltd.* v. *Barclays Bank Ltd.* [1979] 2 Lloyds Rep. 142.

ness by paying the factor.[48] The only reason why a factor would need to give an express notice of the assignment to the debtor would be that the debtor has not been instructed to make payment direct to the factor because the factor has authorised the company to collect debts from its customers as his agent, but the factor suspects that if the company collects the debt, it will not account for the proceeds properly, but will use the proceeds for its own purposes.

An equitable assignment of a debt is complete as soon as it has been made and the debt is in existence, and no notice to the debtor is necessary to complete the assignee's title.[49] If the assigning company subsequently becomes insolvent, the debt or the amount received, if it has been paid to the company, can be segregated from the company's other assets and can be claimed by the factor.[50] An equitable assignee who sues the debtor to recover an assigned debt, if it has not been paid to the company, is admittedly subject to the difficulty that he is compelled to join the company as a co-plaintiff or co-defendant in his action, because the legal title to the debt remains vested in the company. However, this difficulty can easily be overcome in respect of factoring agreements by the assigning company appointing the factor irrevocably to be its agent to bring actions against its trade debtors in the company's name. Such an authority cannot be revoked, because the factor has an interest in exercising it in order to obtain payment of the debts it has purchased.[51]

A factor, like any other assignee of a debt, is exposed to the risk that the debtor may have defences which he could raise in an action brought against the assignor, and which therefore may be raised against the factor as assignee if he sues the debtor. Such defences may be that the transaction giving rise to the debt is void, voidable or terminable by the debtor (*e.g.* because the transaction was illegal, or induced by mistake or misrepresentation, or because the assignor has been guilty of a fundamental breach of contract entitling the debtor to terminate it), or that the debtor is entitled to set off a liquidated claim against the assignor which is already owing, or an unliquidated claim arising under the same transaction as the debt.[52] The debtor can plead the defence of set-off against the assignee only if the right of set-off arises before the debtor received notice of the assignment, unless the set-off arises under the transaction which is the subject of the assignment.[53] Likewise, the debtor does not obtain a discharge for the debt he owes if he pays the assignor or agrees

---

[48] *Re Kent and Sussex Sawmills Ltd.* [1947] Ch. 177.

[49] *Gorringe* v. *Irwell Valley India Rubber and Gutta Percha Works* (1886) 34 Ch.D. 128.

[50] *International Factors Ltd.* v. *Rodriguez* [1979] K.B. 351; *Re Kayford Ltd.* [1975] 1 W.L.R. 279.

[51] *Smart* v. *Sandars* (1848) 5 C.B. 895.

[52] *Stoddart* v. *Union Trust Ltd.* [1912] 1 Q.B. 181; *Young* v. *Kitchin* (1878) 3 Ex.D. 127.

[53] *Christie* v. *Taunton, Delmard, Lane & Co.* [1893] 2 Ch. 175.

with the assignor for the release of the debt or the variation of his obligations after he has received notice of the assignment.[54] The possibility of debtors acquiring rights of set-off or settling with a company which a factor finances is perhaps the most compelling reason why the factor should give early notice to the debtors that their debts have been assigned to the factor under the factoring agreement, or that the factor should at least instruct the debtors to pay their debts to the factor, or alternatively, to pay them to the company acting as agent for the factor to whom the debts now belong.

[54] *Norrish* v. *Marshall* (1821) 5 Madd 475; *Stocks* v. *Dobson* (1853) 4 De.G.M. & G. 11.

III

The Recovery of Bank Advances to Companies

1. INTRODUCTORY

Litigation

The obvious remedy available to a bank or financial institution to recover advances which it has made to a company is to bring an action of debt against the company for the amount of the advance, interest and commission and other charges which the company has contracted to pay. The bank or institution may issue a writ when the advance falls due for repayment and is not repaid, and if interest is payable during the currency of the advance and not merely in a lump sum when the advance becomes due for repayment, or if commission or other charges fall due on an earlier date, the bank or other plaintiff may issue a writ to recover those items when they have become due.

Relatively few actions for the recovery of advances made by banks are defended, and the value of the proceedings initiated by banks to recover advances and other sums due in connection with them lies as much in the power of a writ to constrain the company, guarantor or other defendant to pay the amount claimed, albeit unwillingly, as in the prospect of a judicial ruling on the validity and extent of the bank's rights. The coercive power of a writ is reinforced by the bank's ability to enter judgment against any of the defendants if he fails to acknowledge service of the writ and give notice of an intention to defend the bank's action, or if after service of the statement of claim the defendant fails to serve his defence on the plaintiff within the time allowed.[1] Because the bank's claim will normally be for a liquidated sum which is susceptible of calculation arithmetically, the bank can enter final judgment against a defendant who defaults in either of these ways, and can then immediately issue execution to recover the amount of the judgment and costs.

Set-off by the bank

Commencing an action to recover the amount due to the bank from the company to which the advance was made or from its guar-

[1] R.S.C. Order 13, r. 1(1) and Order 19, r. 2(1).

47

antors is, of course, not the only remedy available to the bank or financial institution. If the bank is itself indebted on another account to the prospective defendant (whether a principal debtor of the bank or a guarantor), and the bank's indebtedness is immediately due or is recoverable by the defendant on demand (*e.g.* a credit balance on a current account), the bank may set off the prospective defendant's indebtedness to it against its own indebtedness to the prospective defendant, and thereby in effect pay itself the whole or part of the amount which is owed to it.[2] This process of set-off is sometimes called the consolidation of accounts, that is, the merger of the prospective defendant's two accounts with the bank on one of which he is in debit and on the other in credit. Consolidation of accounts is a banker's expression and not a legal one, however, and if accounts are to be consolidated in this way by a bank in order to recover an advance from a borrowing company or its guarantor, all the requirements for a set-off must be satisfied. A set-off cannot be effected, therefore, if the advance made by the bank is not yet due for repayment,[3] or if the amount owing will become due only on the fulfilment of a condition or contingency which has not yet happened.[4] If the amount owing from the bank to the borrowing company or its guarantor is not immediately due and payable on demand (*e.g.* a credit balance on a deposit account), the bank cannot effect an immediate set-off against the advance it has made even though it is due for repayment, but the bank may wait until the amount it owes becomes immediately payable and effect a set-off then.

The right of a bank to recover the whole or part of an advance to a company which has become repayable by setting its amount off against a credit balance in favour of the company or its guarantor, is subject to the limitation that the bank cannot assert its right of set-off if at the time when it would otherwise be exercisable, the bank is aware that the credit balance due to the company or its guarantor is held by it or him in trust for or on behalf of a third person, who is therefore entitled to the credit balance in equity.[5] On the other hand, the element of futurity which impedes a set-off when the advance made by the bank to a company is not yet due for repayment does not prevent the bank effecting a set-off if it or the company goes into liquidation, or if the bank's claim is against a guarantor and the bank or the guarantor is in liquidation or bankrupt. This is because the statutory rules applicable in an insolvency situation require set-off to be effected whenever there have been "mutual credits, mutual debts or other mutual dealings" between

[2] *Garnett* v. *McKewan* (1872) L.R. 8 Ex. 10.
[3] *Buckingham & Co.* v. *London and Midland Bank Ltd.* (1895) 12 T.L.R. 70.
[4] *Jeffryes* v. *Agra and Masterman's Bank* (1866) L.R. 2 Eq. 674.
[5] *Re Gross, Ex p. Kingston* (1871) 6 Ch.App. 632; *W. P. Greenhalgh and Sons* v. *Union Bank of Manchester Ltd.* [1924] 2 K.B. 153; *Barclays Bank Ltd.* v. *Quistclose Investments Ltd.* [1970] A.C. 567.

the parties, and the fact that either or both of the amounts owing by and to the bank are not yet due and immediately payable does not prevent them being set off.[6] Moreover, in an insolvency situation set-off is mandatory, and cannot be avoided by a contrary provision in the contract between the parties or by agreement. This does not work to a bank's disadvantage, however, because if the bank is solvent and the borrowing company or guarantor for the advance made to it is not, the insolvency set-off rule can only improve the bank's position; to the extent that the bank sets off its own indebtedness to the company or the guarantor, it pays itself the amount owed by the company in full.

Other remedies

A bank which seeks to recover an advance or other amount which is due to it will therefore first resort to any right of set-off which it may assert, and will initiate litigation against the borrowing company and its guarantors only if the bank has no right of set-off, or if it cannot recover the whole of the amount due to it by exercising such a right. The bank's primary remedies of action and set-off result from the personal liabilities of the borrowing company and its guarantors, but if the indebtedness of the borrowing company is secured, the bank may, additionally or alternatively, realise the securities it holds. Finally, again additionally or alternatively, the bank may as a creditor petition the court to order that the borrowing company shall be wound up compulsorily by the court, and that any of the guarantors for the company's indebtedness shall be made bankrupt, or if they are companies, that they too shall be wound up by the court. These various remedies must now be considered, apart from the bank's right of set-off, which has already been examined.

2. THE ACTION FOR DEBT

The writ accompanied by or indorsed with the statement of claim

An action brought by a bank against a company to recover a loan or advances or an action against a guarantor for the company's indebtedness can be most expeditiously pursued to judgment if the bank serves on the defendant or defendants a copy of its statement of claim at the same time as the writ which initiates the action or, the more usual practice, if the bank indorses its statement of claim on the writ.[7] The statement of claim, whether indorsed on the writ or separate from it, must specify the amount claimed as principal,

---

[6] *National Westminster Bank Ltd.* v. *Halesowen Presswork and Assemblies Ltd.* [1972] A.C. 785.
[7] R.S.C. Order 6, r. 2(1).

49

interest and other charges,[8] but if particulars of the claim have already been delivered in writing to the defendants and exceed 216 words in length, the statement of claim need only state the total amount claimed and the fact that particulars of it have already been delivered to the defendant. The statement of claim must also state that the action will be automatically stayed if the defendants or any of them pay the amount claimed to the bank or its solicitor, together with the banks' fixed costs for issuing and serving the writ and statement of claim, within 14 days after the writ is served.[9]

The statement of claim, whether indorsed on the writ or not, should claim interest on the principal of the loan or advances made by the bank at the rate provided by the contract on which the bank sues and calculated up to the date of the issue of the writ, and the statement of claim should also claim further interest at the same rate from that date until the date when judgment is entered in the action or the principal is previously paid, but such additional interest cannot, of course, yet be quantified.[10] If the principal of the advance does not carry a contractual rate of interest, which is most unlikely in the case of a bank advance, the bank may in its statement of claim include a claim for interest at a rate from time to time fixed by rules of court (currently 15 per cent. per annum) from the date when the principal fell due for payment until the date when the writ was issued, together with further interest from that date until the date of judgment or prior payment of the amount claimed.[11] If compound interest is claimed under the terms of the contract between the bank and the defendants, the calculation of its total amount must be included in the statement of claim, unless written particulars of it have previously been delivered to the defendants.

Interest at the contractual or statutory rate ceases to run when judgment is obtained. Instead interest is thereafter payable on the whole amount for which judgment is entered at a rate which is fixed by regulations and varies from time to time (currently it is 15 per cent. per annum),[12] and the court has no power to alter that rate, even though the contractual rate of interest payable before judgment was higher or lower.[13] If the bank wishes to recover interest at the contractual rate after judgment as well as before, the contract between it and the defendants must expressly so provide[14]; if it does so provide, the bank's statement of claim must state that interest is

---

[8] R.S.C. Order 18, r. 8(4).
[9] R.S.C. Order 6, r. 2(1).
[10] R.S.C. Order 18, r. 8(4).
[11] Supreme Court Act 1981, s.35A(1) and (4) (inserted by Administration of Justice Act 1982, s.15(1) and Sched. 1).
[12] Judgments Act 1883, s.17 (as amended by Administration of Justice Act 1970, s.44).
[13] *Rocco Guiseppe e Figli* v. *Tradex Export* [1983] 3 All E.R. 598.
[14] *Re European Central Ry.*, *Ex p. Oriental Financial Corp.* (1876) 4 Ch.D. 33.

claimed at that rate after judgment as well as beforehand, so that judgment may be entered accordingly.

Application for summary judgment

The advantage to the bank of serving a statement of claim with its writ or, alternatively, indorsing its statement of claim on the writ, is that if the defendant or any of the defendants gives notice of his or its intention to defend the action, the bank may apply to the court on summons for judgment against the defendant in question on the ground that the defendant has no defence to the action.[15] The application must be supported by an affidavit sworn on behalf of the bank by one of its authorised officers or by its solicitor; the affidavit must verify the facts on which the bank's claim is based (which it may do by a statement of the deponent's information and belief if he cannot testify directly to all those facts) and the affidavit must conclude with a statement that the deponent believes that the defendant has no defence to the action.[16]

(1) *Procedure*

The defendant must be served with the summons for summary judgment and the supporting affidavit, and he may file and serve on the bank an affidavit in reply in which he may allege that he has a defence to the bank's claim, specifying it and setting out the facts which he contends establish the defence.[17] A copy of the defendant's affidavit must be served on the bank or its solicitor, and it may then file and serve a further affidavit dealing with the matters raised as a defence in the defendant's affidavit and deposing as to further matters of fact or law which the bank contends make the defence untenable. In fact, it is rarely necessary for the bank to file an affidavit in response to the defendant's affidavit; the original affidavits of the parties should have made the basis of the bank's claim and the intended defence sufficiently apparent for the master or registrar to deal with the application for summary judgment on the hearing.

(2) *Demonstration of a prima facie defence*

On the hearing of the summons the burden of establishing a *prima facie* defence to the bank's claim rests on the defendant, but the court will give leave for it or him to defend if the facts alleged in the affidavit filed in reply to the plaintiff's affidavit are plausible and would, if proved, establish a defence in law, or if the court considers that

---

[15] R.S.C. Order 14, r.1(1).
[16] R.S.C. Order 14, r. 2(1) and (2).
[17] R.S.C. Order 14, r. 4(1).

there is a substantial question of fact to be tried.[18] The court may give the defendant leave to defend the bank's action conditionally or unconditionally, and it has shown an inclination in recent years to give leave only if the defendant pays the whole or part of the amount claimed into court in cases where the defence alleged by the defendant is tenuous or improbable on the facts, and it appears likely that the defendant is merely seeking to delay the action.[19]

(3) Costs

If the court rejects the bank's application for summary judgment, it will usually order that the costs of the application shall be costs in the cause, which means that they shall be paid by whichever party is ordered to pay the costs of the action when judgment is given on the trial, and the costs of the application are dealt with in this way if the court makes no order as to costs when it rejects the application.[20] However, the court will order the plaintiff to pay the costs of the application in any event, if it is satisfied that the plaintiff knew that the defendant had a reasonable defence to plead when the summons for summary judgment was issued and the court consequently gives the defendant leave to defend.[21] Whether an application for summary judgment is successful or not, the dissatisfied party may appeal to the judge in chambers against the master's or registrar's decision,[22] and a further appeal lies from the judge to the Court of Appeal, but in the Chancery division only if the judge or the Court of Appeal has given leave to appeal.[23]

Set-off by a debtor or guarantor

The bank's right of set-off as a means of recovering the whole or part of the amount payable to it in respect of an advance has already been examined, together with the availability of set-off against the borrowing company or against its guarantor. It now remains to consider set-off as a defence on which any of the defendants may rely in an action by the bank to recover an advance or interest or other charges in respect of it. This is of course, set-off operating in the converse direction, where it is the bank's debtor, or a guarantor for the bank's debtor, who seeks to reduce the amount recoverable in the action by relying on a right of set-off.

The Rules of the Supreme Court permit set-off to be pleaded as a

---

[18] R.S.C. Order 14, r. 4(3)); *Yorkshire Banking Co.* v. *Beatson* (1879) 4 C.P.D. 213 (estoppel); *Jones* v. *Stone* [1894] A.C. 122 (estoppel); *Morgan and Sons Ltd.* v. *S. Martin Johnson & Co. Ltd.* [1949] 1 K.B. 107 (equitable set-off).

[19] *Ionian Bank Ltd.* v. *Couvreur* [1969] 1 W.L.R. 781.,

[20] R.S.C. Order 58, r. 1(1).

[21] *Pocock* v. *ADAC Ltd.* [1952] 1 T.L.R.

[22] R.S.C. Order 58, r. 1(1) and r. 3(1).

[23] R.S.C. Order 58, r. 6(1) and (2).

defence to an action whether the amount sought to be set off is an ascertained or liquidated amount or not,[24] but this gives no guidance as to the circumstances in which set-off can be pleaded as a defence. The defence of set-off was originally created by the Insolvent Debtors Act 1729, s.13, which was operative for five years, but was made permanent by the Statute of Set-Off 1735, s.4. The 1729 Act enabled a defendant in an action of debt to set off a debt owed to him by the plaintiff if the two debts were mutual, and this set the limits to the availability of set-off at law. During the eighteenth and nineteenth centuries equity enlarged the number of situations where set-off could be pleaded, whether the plaintiff's claim was a common law one for debt or other liquidated sum, or an equitable claim for a specific sum of money or for an amount which could be quantified in money (*e.g.* the amount for which a fiduciary is accountable or for which he can claim an indemnity).

The Acts of 1729 and 1735 were repealed by the Civil Law Procedure Acts Repeal Act 1877, s.2 and Schedule, but the effect of the rules of law and equity as to set-off have been maintained by the successive Judicature Acts, and are still maintained intact by the Supreme Court Act 1981, s.49(2). The detailed rules governing set-off are heavily overlaid by the broad terms of the latter section, which directs that the corts "shall give the same effect as hitherto . . . to all equitable . . . defences and counterclaims . . . and . . . subject thereto, to all legal claims and demands . . . created by any statute," but beneath this uniform treatment of rights of set-off and counterclaims, the distinctive limits of set-off remain effective. To find these limits resort must be had to the repealed Acts of 1729 and 1735, which still prescribe when set-off is permissible at law, and there must also be taken into account the supplemental rules of equity which extended those circumstances by analogy.

(1) *Comparison of set-off at law and in equity*

Set-off at law is possible when the plaintiff and defendant are mutually indebted, that is, when they have claims against each other for liquidated sums which exist and are immediately due and payable either when the plaintiff commences his action by issuing a writ or when the defendant later pleads the defence of set-off, and those sums must be owing between the parties in the same capacity and the same right. Consequently, a defendant to whom the plaintiff is indebted for a sum which is not due when the defence of set-off is pleaded, but which becomes due before the trial cannot rely on the defence of set-off at law.[25] Under the extended equitable set-off rules, however, the defendant may set off a sum owing to him by the

[24] R.S.C. Order 18, r. 17.
[25] *Crompton* v. *Walker* (1860) 3 E. & E. 321.

plaintiff when the plaintiff's action is commenced even though it is not then due, provided that it becomes due before judgment.[26] Again, a defendant who is sued for a debt which is immediately due and payable may not at law set off a claim for a debt owed to the defendant by a third party which the plaintiff has guaranteed, even if that debt is also immediately due,[27] but in equity the defendant can set off the guaranteed debt against his own indebtedness to the plaintiff.[28] Likewise, if a guarantor of a debt is sued by the creditor, he can set off at law a debt which the creditor owes to the principal debtor, because his guarantee extends only to the amount which the creditor can recover from the principal debtor, and this is diminished by the amount which he is entitled to set off. Additionally, in equity (but not at law) the surety can set off a debt which is owed to him personally by the creditor.[29]

At law it is possible for the defendant to set off a debt owed by the plaintiff which is immediately due and payable to the defendant against the debt owed by the defendant for which the plaintiff sues, but it is not possible for the defendant to set off an amount for which the plaintiff is accountable as a fiduciary for the defendant, or to set off a claim for unliquidated damages, even if it arises under the same transaction as the debt owed to the plaintiff. On the other hand, in equity the defendant can set off an equitable liability of the plaintiff to account to the defendant,[30] and the defendant may also in equity set off a claim for unliquidated damages arising from the same or a related transaction as the one under which the plaintiff's claim arises, but not if the defendant's claim arises under an entirely separate transaction.[31]

(2) Usual situations where set-off is pleaded

When a bank sues a borrowing company or its guarantor, the claims of the defendants by way of set-off which the bank is most likely to meet are:

(a) that the bank is indebted to the defendant in connection with the same or a different transaction, and that the debt owed to the defendant is already due or will become due before the bank obtains judgment against the defendant (*e.g.* a credit balance on a deposit account with the bank which is repay-

---

[26] *White* v. *O'Brien* (1824) 1 Sim. & St. 551; *Maw* v. *Ulyatt* (1861) 31 L.J. Ch. 33.

[27] *Crawford* v. *Stirling* (1802) 4 Esp. 207; *Morley* v. *Inglis* (1837) 4 Bing N.C. 58.

[28] *Jones* v. *Mossop* (1844) 3 Hare 568; *Middleton* v. *Pollock* (1875) L.R. 20 Eq. 515.

[29] *Anglo-Italian Bank Ltd.* v. *Wells* (1878) 38 L.T. 197.

[30] *Freeman* v. *Lomas* (1851) 9 Hare 109; *Stammers* v. *Elliott* (1867) L.R. 4 Eq. 675.

[31] *Agra and Masterman's Bank* v. *Leighton* (1866) L.R. 2 Ex. 56; *Morgan and Son Ltd.* v. *S. Martin Johnson & Co. Ltd.* [1949] 1 K.B. 107; *Hanak* v. *Green* [1958] 2 Q.B. 9; *Gilbert Ash (Northern) Ltd.* v. *Modern Engineering (Bristol) Ltd.* [1974] A.C. 689; *British Anzani (Felixstowe) Ltd.* v. *International Marine Management (UK) Ltd.* [1980] Q.B. 137.

able on a fixed future date or on short notice calling for repayment being given);

(b) that the bank is liable to the defendant for breach of the contract on which the bank sues or under a closely related contract, and the defendant is accordingly entitled to unliquidated damages (*e.g.* a contract for supplemental advances to be made by the bank in addition to the amount advanced under the original loan contract); and

(c) a claim for amounts for which the bank is accountable to the defendant in equity because of a fiduciary relationship between them (*e.g.* income or proceeds of realisation of a security for the defendant's indebtedness which the bank could have recovered but for its default or negligence).

All such claims by the defendant to exercise a right of set-off are sustainable in equity even though only the first of them, (a), is sustainable at law, and then only if the debt owing by the bank is already due when the defence of set-off is pleaded.

(3) *Set-off and counterclaim*

A defendant who is sued on any cause of action may counterclaim in respect of a cause of action which he has against the plaintiff, and the restrictive rules as to set-off do not then apply.[32] Moreover, when the defendant counterclaims for a money claim (whether liquidated or not) in an action brought to enforce a money claim (again whether liquidated or not), and the court upholds both claims, judgment is given for the difference between the amounts awarded to the parties by the court, so that at that stage a set-off is effected by the terms of the court's judgment.[33] It appears at first sight, therefore, that the highly technical rules governing the availability of set-off are of little practical importance if what cannot be set off can be counterclaimed. There is, however, the important difference between set-off and counterclaim that in the situations where legal or equitable set-off is available, the defendant is entitled to plead it as of right as a defence to the plaintiff's action, and the court cannot prevent the defendant from doing this despite the inconvenience of trying the plaintiff's and the defendant's claims together. On the other hand, it is always possible for the court to direct that a counterclaim shall be tried separately from the plaintiff's action, in which case two separate judgments for the amounts awarded to the plaintiff and defendant respectively are given if both claims are successful.

In certain actions the court will not permit the defence of set-off to be pleaded if the plaintiff applies for summary judgment on the

---

[32] R.S.C. Order 15, rule 2(1).
[33] R.S.C. Order 15, r. 2(4).

ground that the defendant has no defence to his action.[34] The court's jurisdiction to give or refuse summary judgment is discretionary, and can therefore be used to exclude certain categories of defence from being pleaded. In actions to recover amounts due to banks under bank loans and advances where the bank sues on a bill of exchange, cheque or promissory note drawn or accepted by the borrowing company or a guarantor of the loan in order to pay or secure the payment of amounts owing to the bank in respect of the loan, the court will only exceptionally allow a defence which does not relate to the validity of the bill, cheque or note to be raised so as to resist an application for summary judgment on the instrument. If the defendant seeks to rely on a right of set-off, he can be given leave to defend only if the amount he seeks to set off is a debt or liquidated sum immediately due and payable to him by the plaintiff bank (*e.g.* the repayment to him of an amount he has paid the plaintiff bank for a consideration which has wholly failed), and he cannot seek to set off an unliquidated claim for damages, whether it arises under the loan transaction or not.[35] Moreover, the defendant cannot even seek to set off a debt or liquidated claim unless he alleges and tenders *prima facie* proof that the plaintiff bank is neither a holder in due course nor even a holder for value of the bill, cheque or promissory note on which it sues.[36]

The reason for the court's refusal to give leave to defend in such cases is that negotiable instruments must be treated in litigation as the equivalent of currency or cash, and consequently, actions between the parties to them where summary judgment is sought must not be impeded by allowing defences to be pleaded which do not relate to the validity of the negotiable instrument itself. The court does not, of course, apply this reasoning if the action on the negotiable instrument goes to trial because the plaintiff does not apply for a summary judgment, or applies for summary judgment unsuccessfully, or if the defendant brings a separate action against the plaintiff in reliance on the material which he is precluded from relying on as a defence.

Set-off where the bank is an assignee

Where a bank sues a borrowing company or its guarantor under a contract for a loan or advances, the rules governing the defence of

---

[34] R.S.C. Order 14, r. 1(1).

[35] *James Lamont and Co. Ltd.* v. *Hyland Ltd.* [1950] 1 K.B. 585; *Brown Shipley and Co. Ltd.* v. *Alicia Hosiery Ltd.* [1966] 1 Lloyds Rep. 668; *Saga of Bond Street Ltd.* v. *Avalon Promotions Ltd.* [1972] 2 Q.B. 325; *Nova (Jersey) Knit Ltd.* v. *Kammgarn Spinnerei GmbH* [1977] 1 W.L.R. 713.

[36] *Oulds* v. *Harrison* (1854) 10 Exch. 572; *Jade International Steel Stahl und Eisen GmbH & Co. K.G.* v. *Robert Nicholas Steels Ltd.* [1978] Q.B. 917.

set-off apply in their normal way. However, if the bank or its specialised subsidiary sues to recover a debt which the company it finances has assigned to it (*e.g.* under a factoring agreement, or where the company creates a mortgage or charge over its trade debts owing from its customers), the debt is owed, not by the company which the bank finances, but by its debtor. In this situation the company's debtor can plead against the bank or its subsidiary the same rights of set-off in law and in equity as it could have pleaded against the company if it had been the plaintiff, subject to the qualification that the debtor cannot plead the right to set off debts incurred by the company to its debtor after he was given notice of the assignment to the bank or its subsidiary, unless those debts arose under the same transaction as the assigned debt.[37]

(1) *Debts arising before notice of assignment*

In determining whether a debt of the company to its debtor under a separate transaction arose or accrued before notice of assignment of the debt owed by the debtor was given to him by the bank or its subsidiary, the material date is not when the company's debt to its debtor becomes payable, but when the company incurred an unconditional obligation to its debtor to pay him a liquidated sum, even though that sum may not be payable until a later date. Consequently, if after the company becomes a creditor of the debtor it acquires goods or services from the debtor at an agreed price with the benefit of a certain length of credit, and before the credit expires the company assigns the debt owed by its debtor to the bank, which gives the debtor notice of the assignment immediately, the debtor can set off the price for the goods or services supplied by it to the company against the debt it now owes the bank, but, of course, only when the period of credit which the debtor gave the company expires. The reason for this is that the company became unconditionally obliged to pay the price to its debtor before notice of assignment to the bank of the debt owed by the debtor to the company was given to him. That obligation arose or accrued when the goods or services were supplied, not when the price for them became payable.

The difficulty in applying the equitable rule as to set-off by a debtor against an assignee in particular situations lies in determining when the debt of the assignor (the company in our case) to the debtor became unconditional. If the assignor's liability to his debtor under a contract is to make a payment only when the debtor has done a certain act (*e.g.* permitted the assignor to possess property for a period for which rent is payable under a lease),[38] or when a certain event has occurred (*e.g.* when calls for unpaid capital have been

---

[37] *Christie* v. *Taunton, Delmard, Lane & Co. Ltd.* [1893] 2 Ch. 175.
[38] *Watson* v. *Mid-Wales Ry.* (1867) L.R. 2 C.P. 593.

made on shares held by the assignor in the debtor company),[39] or when the assignor or the debtor or both of them have terminated the contract under which the debtor's claim arises (*e.g.* agreed compensation payable by the assignor to the debtor on the repudiation of the contract between them and acceptance of the repudiation by the debtor),[40] the assignor's liability becomes unconditional, and the debt owed to the assignor's debtor arises, only when the acts in question have been done or the event in question has occurred. Consequently, even though the assignor's contractual undertaking to make a payment to the debtor is given before notice of the assignment of the debtor's indebtedness to the assignor is given to the debtor by the bank as assignee, the debtor cannot set off the amount payable to him in consequence of that undertaking, unless the assignor's obligation to pay it has become unconditional and therefore a debt before notice of the assignment is given to the debtor.

(2) *Claims under the assigned contract*

The right of a debtor to set off a claim which he has against the assignor of his indebtedness under the same contract or transaction as gave rise to his indebtedness is of an entirely different nature, because the assignee can enforce no greater rights under that contract or transaction than the assignor could have done if he had retained them. Consequently, the debtor can set off against the assignee of the debt he owes the assignor under a contract all liquidated sums payable by the assignor to the debtor under the contract, and also all claims for unliquidated damages which the debtor has against the assignor for breaches of the same contract, whether the liquidated sums accrue or the breaches occur before or after notice of the assignment of the debtor's indebtedness is given to him.[41] However, the debtor's right of set-off against the assignee is confined to claims arising under the transaction in question and, possibly, under closely related transactions entered into by the debtor with the assignor.[42] It is not therefore possible for the debtor to set off against an assignee a claim for unliquidated damages in tort which he has against the assignor for fraudulently inducing the debtor to enter into the contract under which the debtor incurred the indebtedness.[43] This is because such a claim does not arise under the contract; the fraudulent inducement was simply a wrongful act of the assignor, and it preceded the contract and was not done in execution of it.

---

[39] *Christie* v. *Taunton, Delmard, Lane & Co Ltd.* [1893] 2 Ch. 175).

[40] *Business Computers Ltd.* v. *Anglo-African Leasing Co. Ltd.* [1977] 1 W.L.R. 578).

[41] *Re Natal Investment Co., Financial Corporation's Claim* (1868) 3 Ch.App. 355; *Young* v. *Kitchin* (1887) 3 Ex.D. 127.

[42] *British Anzani (Felixstowe) Ltd.* v. *International Marine Management (UK) Ltd.* [1980] Q.B. 137.

[43] *Stoddart* v. *Union Trust Ltd.* [1912] 1 K.B. 181.

(3) *The risks assumed by an assignee*

The rules governing the rights of a debtor to set off debts and claims for damages against an assignee of the debt he owes undoubtedly create an element of risk for a factoring company which takes assignments of trade debts owed to a company which it finances. Without the foreknowledge or consent of the factoring company, the amount which it can collect from the company's debtors may be diminished by the deduction of debts which the company owes them and by claims for damages under their contracts with the company.

A factoring company can nevertheless protect itself against such deductions being made by enquiring whether the debtor claims a right of set-off before accepting an assignment of the debt he owes, and relying on his negative response as estopping him from pleading a right of set-off later. Such enquiries are impracticable in a business context, however, and the most the factor can do in practice is to notify the company's trade debtors of the assignment of their debts as soon as possible after it takes place, or to require the company to include a notice of the general assignment of its trade debts in the invoices it sends to its customers. Most companies are understandably reluctant to advertise their financing arrangements in this way, and so unless the factor gives notice to the company's debtors itself, it carries the whole of the risk.

A sounder alternative for the protection of the factor is for it to require the company to include a further term in its conditions of business. The term will preclude the company's customers from setting off any amounts they owe to the company against any amounts they claim from the company whether such amounts are liquidated or not, and whether they arise under the same or other transactions with the company.

3. THE REALISATION OF SECURITY

The extent of security

In practice banks rely on their right to realise any security they hold for a loan or advance made to a company only as a iast resort after they have exhausted all other means of obtaining payment. If the company is clearly insolvent, and recovery in full from any guarantors of the company's indebtedness is not possible, a bank will, of course, rely on its security, and in particular will do so if the company is in liquidation and the bank has no prospect of recovering the whole, or almost the whole, of the amount owing to it by proving in the liquidation as an ordinary creditor. For this reason it is important for a bank to ensure that the value of the security it takes is sufficient to cover the amount advanced by it when it makes its initial advance, and to check periodically that this is so while the advance and any further amount since borrowed from the bank remain outstanding. The security should also be sufficient to cover the costs incurred by the bank and the costs which are likely to be incurred if the security has to be realised.

(1) *The "all moneys" charge*

The form which any security for advances made by a bank may take is a matter for negotiation with the borrowing company, but if a bank makes a loan other than a modest one for a short period, it will seek to obtain the widest ranging security which is compatible with the continued carrying on of the company's business undertaking. The modern banking practice is to have the company execute a general mortgage or charge over its assets to secure all amounts for which it is from time to time indebted to the bank, whether on an overdrawn account or accounts, or in respect of loans made under separate loan agreements, or in respect of guarantees given by the company for other persons' indebtedness, or in connection with contractual or other obligations of the company to indemnify the bank (*e.g.* in respect of letters of credit issued at the company's request). Such general mortgages or charges, or "all moneys" charges as they are commonly called, create a single, uniform security for all the company's indebtedness to the bank, and consequently it is unnecessary for the bank to call for the creation of special additional security when a particular financial facility is later created for the company. Further charges to secure particular advances are then later called for only if the general charge is not sufficiently comprehensive to extend to assets which the company will acquire by using the new facility (*e.g.* the acquisition of land abroad where a specific charge is required by local law), or when it is useful for the bank to have a means of realising its security quickly and to require the company to account to the bank immediately if the company is empowered to dispose of the subject matter of the security (*e.g.* where shipping documents for goods are released to a customer company under trust letters or trust receipts).

Categories of charges

General or "all moneys" charges created by companies in favour of their banks usually extend to all the company's assets, which are charged by classes, and so far as practicable the charge is made a fixed charge attaching specifically to all the assets of the class which the company owns at the time the charge is created, and also to all assets of the same class which it later acquires.

The company will therefore usually charge to the bank "as a continuing security for the payment of all moneys owed by it to the bank and the discharge of all obligations and liabilities which it incurs to the bank," first, by way of fixed charge, the freehold and leasehold property of the company specified in a schedule to the document creating the charge and also all freehold and leasehold property which the company acquires in the future, together with all buildings, erections and fixtures from time to time in or on such property and all plant, machinery, vehicles, and equipment of the company both present and future (except raw materials, work in progress, finished goods and stock-in-trade); secondly, by way of fixed charge, all stocks, shares, debentures and securities to which the company is entitled in any company, corporation or entity at the date of the charge or subsequently, together with all rights at any time arising or accruing in connection with such investments; thirdly, by way of fixed charge, all book and other debts at any time owing to or acquired by the company; fourthly, by way of fixed charge, the uncalled and unpaid capital of the company from time to time, and also its goodwill, patents, trade marks, registered designs and other industrial property rights registered or owned in the United Kingdom or elsewhere, together with all licences at any time held by the company in respect of industrial property rights; and finally, by way of floating charge, the undertaking and all other property of the company not previously charged or in respect of which such a fixed charge is ineffective.

The reason why the bank takes fixed charges over as many categories of the company's assets as possible is to minimise the impact of the provisions of the Insolvency Act 1986, ss.40, 175 and 245, which give priority to the payment of certain debts of the company over debts secured by a floating charge in the company's liquidation and in a receivership, and which invalidate floating charges given within a certain period before a company goes into liquidation in an insolvent condition or before an administration order is made against it, if the charge is given to secure amounts which are already owing.

(1) *Character of the charges*

If a company executes a document creating charges in favour of its bank in the form described above, or a similar form, the fixed or specific charges it creates over the various classes of its assets may take the form of legal mortgages or charges if the assets are owned by the company when the document creating the charges is executed and, in the case of land and tangible movable property, the document is executed as a deed. Assets of the company acquired after the execution of the document can be subjected to legal mortgages or charges only if the company executes a confirmatory document after their acquisition, but under the original document they are subject to an equitable charge immediately they are acquired, because equity treats the company's attempt to charge them as an agreement to give a legal charge over them on their acquisition which equity will enforce specifically, and the agreement takes effect as an immediate equitable charge.[44] The charge over the company's present and future book debts and over other debts at any time owing to it takes effect as an equitable charge both as regards debts arising after the creation of the charge because of the element of futurity, and as regards debts owing at the date of the charge because the company does not assign them absolutely to the bank and no notice of an assignment is given to the debtors so as to satisfy the requirements of the Law of Property Act 1925, s.136(1). An equitable charge over book and other debts can be specific or fixed, and not merely a floating charge, if it is expressed to be a fixed charge and the company is required to account to the bank for the proceeds of any such debts which is receives.[45]

(2) *Floating charges*

The final component of the charges over a company's assets to secure its indebtedness to a bank creates a floating charge over the remainder of the company's assets which do not belong to a class which has previously been specifically charged. The floating charge comprises primarily the company's current assets (such as raw materials, semi-finished and finished products and stock-in-trade) which are constantly changing in the course of carrying on the company's business, and therefore cannot be subjected to a fixed charge.[46] Assets which are comprised in a floating charge, unlike those subject to a fixed charge, can be disposed of by the company free from the charge if the disposal is made in the ordinary course of the company's business, and the floating charge attaches specifically only to the assets of the kind charged which the company owns when it goes into liquidation, or when a receiver is appointed either by the court or by the bank under a power reserved to it, or when an event occurs which by the terms of the charge is to cause the floating charge to crystallise.[47]

In order to protect the bank against other creditors of the company acquiring fixed charges ranking in priority to the bank's floating charge, the document creating the floating charge normally prohibits the company from creating other charges over any of its assets comprised in the floating charge, if under the general law they would rank in priority to or equally with the floating charge. This provision is effective against other creditors of the company who are aware of it (and not merely of the existence of the bank's floating charge) when they subsequently take fixed charges over the com-

---

[44] *Holroyd* v. *Marshall* (1862) 10 H.L.C. 191; *Tailby* v. *Official Receiver* (1888) 13 App. Cas. 523.
[45] *Siebe Gorman & Co. Ltd.* v. *Barclays Bank Ltd.* [1979] 2 Lloyds Rep. 142.
[46] *Re Bond Worth Ltd.* [1980] Ch. 228.
[47] *Re Woodroffes (Musical Instruments) Ltd.* [1986] Ch. 366; *Re Brightlife Ltd.* [1987] Ch. 200.

pany's assets.[48] On the other hand, if the document creating a floating charge provides for its automatic crystallisation or its crystallisation at the option of the bank on the occurrence of certain events, and the company goes into receivership, the assets of the company comprised in the charge must be applied in paying the company's debts which would be preferential if the company were wound up before paying the amount secured to the bank,[49] and it is impossible to ensure that the bank's crystallised floating charge has priority over those preferential debts by any contractual provision.

Receiverships and sale

The powers of realisation given to mortgagees and chargees by the general law are never adequate to meet the needs of a bank which has taken a charge over the business assets and undertaking of a company. A mortgagee or chargee, whether his security is legal or equitable, may always obtain an order of the court that the property comprised in the security shall be sold, or that a receiver of it shall be appointed either to receive the income or to sell or otherwise realise the property, but the court will order a sale or a receivership only if the borrower has defaulted in paying principal or interest under his loan agreement, or if the subject-matter of the security is in jeopardy and there is a substantial risk of it being lost.

(1) *Statutory powers of realisation*

A bank does not wish to incur the expense and delay involved in seeking an order for sale or the appointment of a receiver by the court, particularly if the company it has financed is insolvent, or is likely to become insolvent. Limited powers of sale and to appoint a receiver of income are conferred on mortgagees and chargees by the Law of Property Act 1925, ss.101, 103, 104 and 109, but these powers are effective only if the security is a legal mortgage or charge executed as a deed, and the powers may be exercised only in a limited range of circumstances, which are insufficient in extent to protect a bank which has financed a trading company. The bank needs to realise its security quickly because of the character of the assets comprised in it, or because the borrowing company is or is likely to become insolvent. Because of the inadequacy of the general law, documents creating a security over a company's business assets for bank advances invariably contain their own detailed provisions defining the circumstances in which the bank may realise its security, the way in which the realisation may be carried out and the way in which the proceeds of realisation shall be applied.

The powers of realisation conferred on a bank by the document

---

[48] *Re Castell and Brown Ltd.* [1898] 1 Ch. 315; *Wilson* v. *Kelland* [1910] 2 Ch. 306.
[49] Insolvency Act 1986, s.40(1) and (2).

63

which charges the borrowing company's assets are by the terms of the document usually made exercisable immediately on the company committing an act of default or on the occurrence of an event of default as defined by any of the loan agreements entered into by it with the bank, or on the bank demanding payment of the amount which is owing and immediately payable to it under all or any of the loan agreements which it has entered into with the company. The acts or events of default or the circumstances in which the amount owing to the bank becomes immediately payable are defined by separate loan agreements made with the company, and they may be different in different loan agreements if the company has entered into several separate agreements with its bank in order to finance different projects or developments. If the company has executed only a single document creating a charge or charges over its assets to secure "all moneys" owed by it to the bank, the powers of realisation which the bank may exercise will nevertheless be uniform, and the loan agreements made with the company are resorted to only to discover when those powers may be exercised.

When the bank's powers of realisation have become exercisable, the document charging the company's assets usually empowers the bank to sell or otherwise realise all or any of the company's assets charged to it, and to exercise the powers of realisation conferred on legal mortgagees by the Law of Property Act 1925 for this purpose. More important than this, however, the bank is also empowered to appoint a receiver or several receivers of the whole or any part of the company's assets charged to it and to do this by instruments of appointment signed by a director or senior officer of the bank; the bank is also empowered to remove, replace or add to the number of such receivers and to fix the receivers' remuneration, and it is declared that each receiver appointed by the bank shall be deemed to be the agent of the company, which shall be solely responsible for his acts and omissions. This latter provision is necessary because in its absence the receiver would be the agent of the bank and it would be accountable for losses caused by the receiver's defaults,[50] except where the receiver is appointed in respect of the whole or substantially the whole of the company's assets under a general or floating charge over them or several such charges in combination, when the receiver, known as an administrative receiver, is deemed to be the agent of the company.[51] A provision in an instrument charging the company's assets which provides that a receiver appointed by the holder of the charge shall be the agent of the company is not wholly effective to put the burden of losses resulting from his acts on the company, however. The receiver owes the company a duty to act with due skill and care in carrying out his functions and in exercising

---

[50] *Deyes* v. *Wood* [1911] 1 K.B. 806.
[51] Insolvency Act 1986, s.44(1).

the powers conferred on him by the document under which he was appointed; if he fails to do so, he is liable to the company in damages for the loss it suffers as a result, and the bank which appointed him also will be liable if the receiver acted on its specific instructions (e.g. if he sells the company's assets at an undervalue).[52] The receiver's status as an agent of the company is, nevertheless, not a real agency in the sense that he is appointed to protect the company's interests; neither the receiver nor the bank need have primary regard to those interests, and neither of them is liable to the company if the receiver on the bank's directions realises the company's assets in order to discharge its indebtedness to the bank when a postponement of the realisation might have resulted in that indebtedness being discharged without the company's undertaking being broken up.[53]

(2) *Powers of a receiver*

The document which charges the borrowing company's assets usually sets out the powers of realisation which may be exercised by a receiver appointed by the bank, and these are expressed in the widest terms so as to enable the receiver to do every conceivable act which may be necessary to convert the company's assets into cash and to pay the amount owing to the bank together with the costs of realisation and the receiver's remuneration. The powers expressly conferred on the receiver by documents creating charges include powers to take possession of, collect and get in any of the company's assets charged to the bank; to exercise all the powers of a holder of investments and securities which are charged; to bring or defend litigation in the company's name or otherwise; to carry on, manage, dispose of, reconstruct, expand or merge the business undertaking of the company or any parts of it; to borrow in the company's name and on its behalf, and to charge any of the assets subject to the charge with such borrowings; to sell, lease or otherwise dispose of any of the assets of the company comprised in the charge on such terms and conditions and for such consideration as the receiver thinks fit; to appoint managers, agents and employees for the purpose of realising the company's assets and to pay them such remuneration as the receiver thinks fit; to enter into compromises and arrangements in the company's name and on its behalf for the purpose of realising its assets or exercising the powers conferred on the receiver; and to execute any documents or deeds on behalf of the company or as its attorney, and to do all such other acts and things as the receiver considers incidental to the exercise of the powers conferred on him. The appointment of the receiver as the company's attorney is usually declared to be irrevocable, and to operate as a

---

[52] *Standard Chartered Bank Ltd.* v. *Walker* [1982] 1 W.L.R. 1410.
[53] *Gomba Holdings UK Ltd.* v. *Homan* [1986] 1 W.L.R. 1301.

general power of attorney under s.10 of the Powers of Attorney Act 1971.

The express powers of a receiver are sufficient in most situations for him to carry through a receivership without the need to apply to the court for directions, but by statute[54] he can apply for such directions as to the performance of his functions, and his ability to do so is useful when he is in doubt as to the exact scope of his express powers, or when the assets of the company comprised in the charge to the bank are of an unusual character, or can be converted into cash only by the receiver entering into a transaction on abnormal terms.

(3) *Impact of the Insolvency Act 1986*

The Insolvency Act 1986 has affected receiverships of company's assets and undertakings in a number of respects, but has not fundamentally altered the way in which a bank will realise its security by means of appointing a receiver. If a bank appoints a receiver of the whole or substantially the whole of a company's property under a charge which, as created, was a floating charge, or under such a charge and any other securities (*e.g.* fixed charges over the company's remaining assets), the receiver is known as an administrative receiver, and he must be qualified professionally to be an insolvency practitioner and be currently authorised to practise as such.[55]

Administrative receivers are invested with statutory powers to fulfil their functions, and this is in addition to the powers conferred on them by the documents which create the charge or charges which they are appointed to realise, but the statutory powers may be excluded or modified by those documents; the staturory powers are similar to the powers which are usually expressly conferred on receivers by documents creating charges over companies' assets in favour of banks.[56] If a bank takes a charge over a class or classes of a company's assets or over a specific property, so that a receiver appointed by the bank to realise the charge is not an administrative receiver, the powers of an administrative receiver can be conferred on him by incorporating those powers by reference to the statutory powers in the document creating the charge.

Finally, an administrative receiver is empowered by the Insolvency Act 1986 to dispose of any property of the company which is comprised in any mortgage or other security which has priority over the charge or charges under which the receiver was appointed; however, he may do this only if the court gives him leave on the ground that the disposal would be likely to lead to a more advantageous realisation of the company's assets than would otherwise be possible

---

[54] Insolvency Act 1986, s.35.
[55] Insolvency Act 1986, s.29(2), s.230(2), s.251, s.388(1) and s.390.
[56] *Ibid.*, s.42(1) and Sched. 1.

(*e.g.* because the mortgaged property can be sold for a higher price if it is sold together with other assets which the receiver proposes to sell), and the proceeds of sale of the morgaged property must be applied primarily in discharging the mortgage or security which is overreached.[57]

Syndicated loans

When a loan is made by a syndicate of banks, each contributing its agreed share of the total amount advanced on uniform terms binding on all the banks, any charges over assets of the company to secure the syndicated loan must be created by the loan agreement entered into by the banks with the company, or by a contemporaneous document. The nature and extent of the security and the powers of the banks to realise the charges will be negotiated for the particular syndicated loan, and it will not be possible for the banks to rely on any security which the company has already given them individually for its indebtedness to them alone. The terms of the security given to individual banks will be different, and the security given to each bank may extend to different classes of assets from those on which the syndicated loan is charged. The need for a uniform security for the syndicated loan will also necessitate an agreement between the participating banks specifying whether their claims for repayment of other advances made by them individually to the borrowing company shall rank equally with, or in priority to, or after their respective claims for payment out of the security for the syndicated loan.

The banks which join in a syndicated loan may agree between themselves whatever they wish as to the way in which the powers of realisation of the charge or charges created by the syndicated loan agreement shall be exercised. It is possible at one extreme for each participating bank to be given power by the syndicated loan agreement to act on its own account alone to recover the amount payable to it by the borrowing company when an act or event of default has occurred. At the other extreme, the lead bank alone may be empowered to act by demanding immediate repayment of the whole of the syndicated loan by the company, and by exercising the powers of realisation conferred by the loan agreement when an act or event of default has occurred. A middle position, which is often taken in practice, is for the loan agreement to empower the lead bank alone to realise the security for the whole of the syndicated loan, but for the participating banks to agree between themselves that it shall do so only if the banks entitled to a specified percentage of the total amount of the loan concur in deciding that the lead bank shall act, or if banks entitled to a specified percentage of the loan require the

[57] *Ibid.*, s.43(1)–(3) and (5).

lead bank to act. In determining whether banks with a sufficient fraction of their total interests concur in deciding on realisation, the share of the total loan to which the lead bank is itself entitled (often the largest share) must, of course, be taken into account.

Where the lead bank requires the concurrence of other participating banks for the exercise of the powers of realisation conferred on it, it is always given extensive powers to take possession or control of assets of the borrowing company on its own initiative, or by means of a receiver appointed by it, so as to conserve the assets comprised in the security for the syndicated loan until a decision on realisation can be taken, and often this power of conservation is accompanied by a power to appoint a manager of the company's business undertaking for the time being.

4. LIQUIDATION AND ADMINISTRATION ORDERS

Creditors' winding-up petitions

A bank which has made advances to a company can, as a creditor, petition the court to order that the company shall be wound up, and the ground for a winding-up order on which the bank relies will invariably be that the company is unable to pay its debts.[58] A company's inability to pay its debts may be proved without the need to establish that the company cannot pay its debts generally as they fall due, or that the company's liabilities exceed its assets. The petitioning creditor can prove the company's insolvency instead by serving a written demand on the company in the form prescribed by regulations requiring it to pay a specified amount of indebtedness (exceeding £750) which is immediately due and payable to the creditor, and by the company neglecting for three weeks thereafter to pay that amount or to secure or compound for it to the reasonable satisfaction of the creditor.[59] This is the way in which the insolvency of a company is normally established on the hearing of a creditor's winding-up petition.

It is unnecessary for a bank or any other creditor of a company to bring an action of debt for the amount it owes the creditor and to obtain judgment against the company before presenting a winding-up petition. Nevertheless, if a bank or other creditor anticipates that the company will plead a defence to its claim which the court will not dismiss as baseless, it should obtain judgment against the company before petitioning, and this should occasion little delay if the bank or other creditor obtains a default judgment or makes a successful application to enter judgment summarily in the absence of a defence to its claim. The reason why the bank or creditor should do

---

[58] Insolvency Act 1986, s.122(1) and s.124(1).
[59] s.123(1).

this is that the court will not determine the validity of *bona fide* defences raised by the company on the hearing of a creditors' winding-up petition, but will dismiss the petition and leave the petitioner to seek a judgment in a separate action before presenting a new petition based on his judgment debt. The court's reluctance to try the merits of the petitioning creditor's claim on the hearing of a winding-up petition is because such a trial will necessitate the adjournment of the hearing of the petition, and this will prevent other creditors presenting winding-up petitions meanwhile and will also make it uncertain whether the directors of the company may lawfully continue to carry on its business.[60] If a creditor obtains judgment against the company for his debt before presenting a winding-up petition, the company will of course, be estopped from pleading as a defence to the petition any defence which it could have pleaded or did plead unsuccessfully to the action, and so the creditor will be certain to obtain a winding-up order, unless the judgment debt has been paid or a majority in value of the company's creditors oppose a winding-up order being made.

Banks do rely on winding-up proceedings as a means of recovering unsecured loans from a borrowing company, but rarely do so when the amount owed by the company is adequately secured. If a bank realises its security by appointing a receiver or otherwise, it is solely in control of the realisation of the company's assets, and it may be able to obtain a better price on the sale of the assets comprised in its security than a liquidator, who is an officer of the court over whom the bank has no control. The bank's priority as a secured creditor is theoretically as well maintained in a liquidation as in a receivership, but the bank is dependent for the proper realisation of its security on the resourcefulness and ability of the liquidator, who may well not be its nominee and whose duties are in any case owed to the generality of the company's creditors (in particular its unsecured creditors) and not primarily to the bank. Because of this, receiverships are of more practical value to banks than liquidations, and even where a liquidation has been initiated by other creditors or by the shareholders of the company resolving to wind it up voluntarily, a bank may still intervene and appoint a receiver to realise the company's assets under the provisions of the document creating its security or under the general law. The receiver will then be entitled to recover the company's assets subject to the bank's charge from the liquidator and to realise them for the bank's benefit.

Administration orders

The alternative form of insolvency proceeding made available to creditors of companies by the Insolvency Act 1986, the administra-

---

[60] *Re Boston Timber Fabrications Ltd.* [1984] B.C.L.C. 328.

tion order, has few attractions for banks which hold securities over the whole of the assets of a company, or over a substantial part of its assets. The purpose of an administration order is to enable the administrator appointed by the court to re-establish the company's business on a sound and solvent basis, or to give effect to a compromise or arrangement between the company and its creditors, or to realise the assets of a company more beneficially for its creditors than in a winding-up.

The rights and powers of its individual creditors to recover what is owed to them and to realise their securities for the purpose are necessarily deferred while an application for an administration order is pending and while the order is in force.[61] Banks prefer not to be bound by collective proceedings of this kind, and to retain their freedom to take individual action to recover what is owed to them and to realise any security they hold. If a bank has a floating charge over the whole or substantially the whole of the assets of the company, it can prevent an administration order being made by appointing an administrative receiver of the company's assets and undertaking before an order is made.[62] If its security is not so extensive and is confined to specific assets of the company or to a class or classes of those assets, the bank has no statutory right to resist the making of an administration order, but it should ensure that by the terms of its agreement with the company it is empowered to take effective steps to recover the amount which the company owes it, or to realise its security for that amount, when there is any risk of either winding-up proceedings or proceedings for an administration order being initiated.

---

[61] Insolvency Act 1986, ss.10 and 11.
[62] *Ibid.*, s.9(3) and s.10(1) and (2).

IV

Bank Finance for Groups of Companies

In the preceding Chapters the various ways in which banks and their specialised subsidiaries assist individual companies by the provision of finance have been surveyed in detail, and the implicit assumption has been made that the company for which finance is provided alone benefits by it and (apart from guarantors) is alone liable for repayment of the loan or advance. The somewhat different situation must now be considered where a bank, either with or without a contractual commitment, finances a group of companies which carry on their operations under the leadership of a parent company at the head of the group. In this situation the rules of law which have already been discussed apply to the individual financing transactions with members of the group, but these rules are modified in their practical application by other considerations resulting from the bank's appraisal and treatment of the group as a single economic and commercial unit. This Chapter, relating to the financing of groups of companies, will therefore be concerned, first with the legal character of the relationship between the companies comprised in a group, secondly, with the structuring of bank financing of the group, thirdly, with the contractual modifications which need to be made to the legal rules which would otherwise apply when a bank finances group companies, and, finally, with the enforcement of the liabilities of companies in a group by a bank which has financed them.

1. THE LEGAL CHARACTER OF THE GROUP

Definition

The definition of a parent or holding company and a subsidiary in the Companies Act 1985, s.736 (derived from the Companies Act 1948, s.150, without alteration) was originally devised in connection with the requirements of the Companies Act 1948 that a holding company should prepare group accounts annually, and should lay copies of them with its own annual balance sheet and profit and loss account before a general meeting of its shareholders each year and deliver a copy of those group accounts together with its own annual accounts to the Registrar of Companies.[1] The definition is also used

---

[1] Companies Act 1948, ss.150 and 151; Companies Act 1985, s.229(1) and s.241(1) and (3).

in the Companies Act 1985 in connection with a wide range of its prescriptions which deal with other matters than group accounts. It nevertheless retains its original character of a precise, immediately applicable criterion which takes only readily ascertainable and objective factors into account. A company is the subsidiary of another company (its holding or parent company) only if:

(a) the other company is a member (*i.e.* a registered shareholder) of it and controls (by voting power, contract or otherwise) the appointment or removal of a majority of the company's directors; or

(b) the other company holds more than half in nominal value of the company's issued equity share capital, that is, its issued share capital other than shares which carry the right to participate in its profits and in its assets in a liquidation only to a limited extent (*i.e.* preference shares issued on normal terms); or

(c) the company is, under (a) or (b), the subsidiary of a third company which is itself the subsidiary of the other company.[2]

The basic simplicity of the definition is qualified only by a few additional provisions which exclude from consideration shares held in the subsidiary and powers exercisable in relation to it which belong to the potential parent company in a fiduciary capacity. The definition serves its original purpose excellently, namely, to determine when a company must prepare group accounts, but it does not work equally as well when applied in other contexts by the Companies Act 1985, for example, to determine whether a company may acquire shares in a company which may be its parent company, or may assist financially in the acquisition by a third person of such shares.

The reason why the statutory definition of a parent company and its subsidiary is not satisfactory for all purposes is that it does not have regard to the real working relationship between the two companies, and in particular does not take into account whether the board of directors of the parent company can and does determine the business policy of the subsidiary. Such a functional definition would inevitably be more general than the one in the Companies Act 1985, and would therefore make it less certain in particular cases whether the legal relationship of parent company and subsidiary existed. This is exemplified by the German legislation of 1965 governing public companies, which provides that a company is the subsidiary or subordinate company of another if the other can exercise a controlling influence over it, either directly or indirectly, and it is presumed that such a controlling influence exists if more than half of the subsidiary's issued share capital is held by the parent com-

---

[2] Companies Act 1985, s.736(1) to (3) and s.744.

pany, but the presumption can be disproved from the facts. Further-more, companies form a group under German law only if the subsidiaries' affairs are conducted under the unified leadership of the parent company, in other words, if the parent company not only has power to control its subsidiaries' affairs, but also actually does so.

No body of rules governing the group relationship

The fact that British law contains merely an accounting definition of a parent company and a subsidiary has not prevented the Companies Act 1985 from making use of the formal relationship between the two companies as a convenient shorthand formula when it extends a rule applicable to a single company (*e.g.* the prohibition on a company making loans to its directors) to other companies in the same group, and this is all that the Act has done. There is, therefore, no separate and self-contained body of rules in the Companies Act 1985 dealing with groups of companies, the internal relationship between companies in a group and the rights and liabilities of a group of companies in relation to outsiders. A group of companies in British law is not a legal entity in itself; it is simply an aggregation of separate companies, each having its own separate rights and liabilities, as though there were no special legal relationship between them. There are therefore no such things as group assets and group liabilities (although they figure as such for accounting purposes only in group accounts); the legality of an act of a company which belongs to a group or of its board of directors is judged as though the company were an independent concern interested only in carrying on its own business operations for its own exclusive benefit; the board of directors of a parent company has no powers conferred by law to direct or instruct the board of its subsidiary how the subsidiary's affairs shall be conducted. Any influence which the directors of a parent company exercise over its subsidiary's directors is attributable to the parent company's majority shareholding in the subsidiary, and to the fact that usually a parent company can cast a majority of the votes at a general meeting of its subsidiary, and can therefore appoint and remove its subsidiary's directors.

The courts have made only limited inroads on the treatment of subsidiary companies as separate and independent legal entities from thir parent companies. This has been done in two cases where a group company held assets which were used exclusively by another group company for the purpose of its business undertaking, and the company holding the assets was held to be a nominee or trustee for the other company, which was therefore treated as the equitable, beneficial owner of the assets.[3] The Court of Appeal has

---

[3] *Smith, Stone and Knight Ltd.* v. *Birmingham Corp.* [1939] 3 All E.R. 116; *D.H.N. Food Distributors Ltd.* v. *London Borough of Tower Hamlets* [1976] 1 W.L.R. 852.

also exceptionally held that when a British wholly-owned subsidiary of an American parent company carried on business in the United Kingdom under the detailed direction of the American parent, the parent itself carried on business in the United Kingdom for tax purposes, using the subsidiary as its agent.[4] These cases are the exception rather than the rule, however.

Propriety of transactions by group companies

When the courts have had to consider the lawfulness of a transaction entered into by a group company, they have shown no elasticity at all in identifying the interests of the company with those of other group companies, and they have ruled that a group company's directors may only properly enter into a transaction on its behalf if they intend to benefit that company itself. If they intend instead to benefit another company or other companies in the group, but the company of which they are directors will not benefit at all, they act improperly and the transaction is not validated, and they are not relieved from liability for breach of duty to their company, by the fact that they intend to benefit the group as a whole.

In one such case,[5] where a subsidiary company guaranteed a bank loan to another company in the same group and mortgaged its assets to secure it, the court held that the guarantee and mortgage could not be invalidated on the ground that it was *ultra vires* the subsidiary, because it had power to give guarantees and security for other persons' debts by its memorandum of association and this obviously included other companies in the same group. Nevertheless, the guarantee and mortgage in this case would have been voidable by the subsidiary if its directors had given them exclusively for the benefit of the other group company, for the directors would then have abused their powers as directors of the subsidiary. However, in that event the guarantee and mortgage would not be set aside against the bank if it was unaware of the directors' intentions when the transaction was negotiated, because of the protection given by equity to third parties who give value and act in good faith. The evidence in the case showed that the bank loan was made to enable the borrowing company to carry out a development which would benefit all the companies in the group, including the subsidiary which had given the guarantee and mortgage. Consequently, the acts of the subsidiary's directors were valid, because they had acted in the interests of their own company, although not exclusively so.

In a more recent case, *Rolled Steel Products (Holdings) Ltd.* v. *British Steel Corp.*,[6] on the other hand, the Court of Appeal held invalid a

---

[4] *Firestone Tyre and Rubber Co. Ltd.* v. *Lewellin* [1956] 1 W.L.R. 352 and [1957] 1 W.L.R. 464.

[5] *Charterbridge Corp. Ltd.* v. *Lloyds Bank Ltd.* [1970] Ch. 62.

[6] [1986] Ch. 246.

guarantee and mortgage to secure a company's indebtedness to British Steel Corporation given in the name of another company by its managing director and majority shareholder, who was also the sole director and beneficial owner of the whole of the issued capital of the debtor company. The Court of Appeal (overruling Vinelott J. on this point) held that the guarantee and mortgage could not be held *ultra vires* the company which gave them, because they were within its express powers conferred by its memorandum of association. The guarantee and mortgage were nevertheless given in breach of the managing director's duty to act in the interests of that company, because it obtained no benefit, and was not intended to benefit, by them being given. Since British Steel Corporation knew this to be so, it could not enforce the guarantee or the mortgage as a person acting in good faith. This case did not involve two companies in the same group, of course; the managing director of the guarantor company was simply the person who held all the issued capital of the debtor company. The same principle would nevertheless have been applied if the guarantor company had been a subsidiary or a fellow subsidiary of the debtor company, and had no interest which would have been served by giving the guarantee and mortgage.

It does not always follow that a security given by a subsidiary for a loan to its parent company or to a fellow subsidiary will be set aside in equity as an abuse of the powers of the subsidiary's directors. If the loan is made to a parent company so that it may re-lend the money to its operating subsidiaries, and the subsidiary which gives the guarantee or mortgage receives a substantial fraction of the total amount advanced, the loan will have been made for its benefit as well as that of other companies in the group, and the guarantee or mortgage will therefore be valid. One is on less certain ground when the subsidiary receives no part of the amount advanced, or when it gives a guarantee or mortgage to secure an advance previously made to its parent company or to a fellow subsidiary without security. In either of those situations the subsidiary would appear to obtain no benefit from giving a guarantee or mortgage to secure the other company's debt, but evidence may be given that on the facts of the particular case the subsidiary did obtain a material benefit, or at least, was intended by its directors to do so, and the guarantee or mortgage will then be enforceable.

Where a parent company guarantees a loan made to its subsidiary or subsidiaries or mortgages its assets as security, it would seem that it will always obtain a benefit, because the value of its investment in the subsidiary or subsidiaries is improved or preserved. It does not follow, however, that a guarantee by a parent company of its subsidiary's existing unsecured indebtedness, or a mortgage given by a parent company to secure such indebtedness, is necessarily of any benefit to the parent company. The result of giving the security may be merely that the parent company's own asset position is made worse, and it would seem that to validate the guarantee or mortgage evidence would be needed to show that giving the guarantee or mortgage was indispensible to preserve the subsidiary as a going concern.

2. STRUCTURE OF BANK FINANCING OF A GROUP

The group as an economic and commercial unit

Because the law insists on treating each company in a group as a separate and independent legal entity and has no such concepts as group objects or purposes and group assets and liabilities (except for accounting purposes), it follows that in law each loan or advance made by a bank to a group company must be treated as an isolated transaction. If a group company guarantees or gives security for a bank loan or advance to another group company, that, too, must be treated as an isolated transaction, and its validity, effectiveness and effect will be determined accordingly.

To a considerable extent banks can overcome the artificial barriers which the law sets up between group companies. In negotiating financial facilities for the group and its constituent companies the bank treats the group as a single economic or commercial unit. When settling the legal documentation for group financing the bank must bear in mind the legal separation of group companies from one another, but by appropriate arrangement it is usually possible to bind all or most companies in the group by the financing arrangements made for it. This is particularly so where all or most of the subsidiaries in a group are wholly-owned by its parent company, that is, the whole of the issued share capital of the subsidiaries in the group is owned beneficially by the parent company. Even where the parent company has only a majority holding of the subsidiaries' equity share capital (whether 51, 75 or 90 per cent.) and there are outside minority shareholders who hold the balance of the subsidiaries' issued share capital, the parent company may run the group as an integrated unit, and its financing by bank advances can be modelled accordingly.

(1) *Investment groups*

The only situation where group companies are financed wholly separately and where it is dangerous to attempt to bind all group companies by financing arrangements made with one of them, is where the parent company treats its holdings in its subsidiaries merely as investments, and leaves the boards of directors of the subsidiaries to manage their respective businesses as they think fit without interference by the parent company. The relationship of parent company and subsidiary is then either accidental or incidental to a wider investment plan. This situation is, in fact, rare, because companies which invest in other companies whose managements they do not wish to control, do not normally take majority holdings of equity share capital, but spread their investments wider, usually holding no more than 20 per cent. of the ordinary shares of any one company in which they invest, and often much less.

(2) *Integrated groups of companies*

Where an integrated group of companies is established under the overall direction of the board of directors of the parent company of the group, whether this comes about by the parent company forming operational subsidiaries or by it acquiring controlling shareholdings in existing companies by acquisitions or takeovers, the group is seen by a bank which finances it as an integrated whole and the group companies which are members of the group as mutually dependent. Consequently, financing arrangements are made for the group as a whole, and a bank which is approached for finance to assist the operations of part of the group, or to enable new developments or projects by particular group companies, inevitably looks at the financial position of the whole group as well as that of the borrowing company in deciding whether to make a loan or advance and, if so, on what terms. When making its decision the bank relies on the group accounts prepared annually by the parent company and recent group management accounts as much as it relies on the accounts of the borrowing company.

This does not, of course, preclude the bank from requiring a borrowing subsidiary or subsidiaries to be restructured by the parent company if the present capitalisation, earnings or assets of the company or companies are not well organised to accommodate the finance which is sought, but this is done purely for commercial reasons so as to ensure that the borrowing company will generate sufficient profits to service an advance made to it, and will have sufficient assets at the appropriate time to repay the advance. The bank does not do this because those earnings and assets will be the only means by which it can ensure that it is repaid the advance with interest, commission and costs. The barriers which the law sets up between companies in the same group can usually be overcome without difficulty by the parent company, or all or a section of the companies in the group, joining in the contractual arrangements made with the group company whose operations are to be financed so as to make them all liable for repayment of the advance and to make their assets available to satisfy the borrowing company's obligations. The distinct advantage to the group of all the group companies or the major ones among them joining in the contractual arrangements is that the borrowing company then obtains better terms from the bank in respect of interest rates, repayment by instalments, maturity dates, etc.

Short term loans

Short term loans made to companies in a group are usually made to the company whose current operations are thereby financed, and if that company's credit is sound, its parent company is either not called on to guarantee repayment of the loan, or the bank is content with a comfort letter from the parent company which states that it is the parent company's intention to support the borrowing company financially, or that it intends to make sufficient resources available to enable the borrowing company to continue trading on its present scale. Comfort letters do not create binding legal obligations, and they are, in any case, phrased in too vague and general terms to be legally binding as contracts.

If a parent company gives a comfort letter when its board knows that it does not intend to support the subsidiary financially or that it does not have the means to do so, the parent company and its directors would, despite the absence of a contract, be liable to a bank which is thereby induced to lend to the subsidiary, and the loss suffered by the bank would be recoverable in an action for the tort of deceit. But if a parent company is prevented from supporting its subsidiary by unforeseen circumstances, such as Government intervention in its affairs, and the parent company refuses to renew a comfort letter or simply fails to support the subsidiary, the parent company and its directors are not guilty of fraud, and the bank cannot sue them in tort or proceed against them in the liquidation of the subsidiary.[7]

Short term loans for the present purpose may be taken as including overdraft facilities, loans made for not more than one year, obligations to reimburse a bank in connection with letters of credit or guarantees issued by the bank at a group company's request, and advances made by a bank accepting, purchasing or discounting bills of exchange or promissory notes issued by a group company. These are, in fact, the only kinds of transactions where a bank is usually willing to give financial assistance on the credit of a group company without the concurrence of all or some of the other companies in the group.

Medium and long term loans

Because of the greater time scale and therefore the greater risk of default by a subsidiary for which medium or long term finance is made available, both commercial banks and merchant banks usually require the subsidiary's parent company and often other subsidiaries in the same group to enter into contractual commit-

---

[7] *Re Augustus Barnett and Son Ltd.* [1986] B.C.L.C. 170.

ments to ensure that the advance made by the bank is repaid, and that interest, commission and the bank's costs and expenses are also duly paid. This can be achieved in one of two ways.

(1) *Direct financing of subsidiaries*

The first alternative is for the bank to make the loan or advance to the subsidiary which is to use it under a loan agreement with the subsidiary by which it contracts to repay the loan with interest, commission and costs, and also mortgages or charges specific assets or classes of its assets to the bank, and charges its remaining assets by way of a floating charge as security for its obligations. The subsidiary's commitments to the bank are then supported by the parent company and some or all of its other subsidiaries executing contemporaneously a contract of guarantee by which they respectively undertake that the borrowing subsidiary's obligations to the bank will be fulfilled. If the bank requires the guarantees to be secured (as it usually does) the parent company and the subsidiaries which are guarantors also execute a document by which they charge specific assets or classes of their assets with amounts payable to the bank under the guarantees they have given, and it is also usual for the parent company and the guarantor subsidiaries to create floating charges over their remaining assets as additional security.

The result of an arrangement of this kind is that the parent company and some or all of its subsidiaries are contractually bound to repay the advance made by the bank with interest, commission and expenses, and the borrowing subsidiary and all of the other companies in the group which give guarantees to the bank have also charged most or all of their respective assets as a cumulative security for the amount payable to the bank. Needless to say, care should be taken to identify correctly the company to which the loan or advance is made and the other companies which give guarantees, and also to identify correctly the various assets which are charged as security for the loan and the guarantees, but if a mistake is made in this respect despite the parties' clear intentions, the court will rectify the documents which they have executed.[8]

(2) *Indirect financing of subsidiaries*

The alternative way in which bank finance may be channelled to the subsidiary or subsidiaries which need it is for the loan to be made by the bank to the parent company of the group, which then lends the money on to the subsidiary or subsidiaries on terms which are satisfactory for the internal management of the group, or simply as an advance made to the subsidiary or subsidiaries which will be repaid in such instalments and at such rate or interest as the board

[8] *Amalgamated Investment and Property Co. Ltd.* v. *Texas Commerce International Bank Ltd.* [1982] Q.B. 84.

of directors of the parent company decides. The parent company's borrowing from the bank will then be guaranteed and secured on its own and all or some of its subsidiaries' assets in a similar manner to that employed when a subsidiary borrows from the bank with the support of guarantees and mortgages by its parent company and fellow subsidiaries. Consequently, the contractual commitments which the bank has for repayment of the loan and its security for repayment will be substantially the same, whether subsidiaries themselves borrow from the bank with the support of other group companies, or whether the loan is made to the parent company of the group and re-loaned by it to its subsidiaries which need the money.

A minor variation on the method of financing a group of companies by a bank making a loan to the parent company of the group for onward lending to its subsidiaries is for the loan to be made to a specially incorporated company which is formed as a subsidiary of the parent company for the purpose of borrowing outside the group in order to re-lend internally to group companies. The obligations of such a specially formed borrowing subsidiary are then guaranteed by the parent company and all or some of its other subsidiaries and secured on their respective assets.

(3) *Composite guarantees and security*

It has become the practice of banks in recent years to require the parent company and all or most of the subsidiaries of a group to which it makes medium or long term loans to execute a document containing cross-guarantees by each of the companies in the group of the obligations of each of the other group companies, and also to require them to give mortgages or charges over the respective assets of all of those companies (including floating charges over their assets which are not specifically charged) to secure their collective guarantees. Often this composite document of guarantee and charge, like an "all moneys" charge given by an individual company, is extended to include an undertaking by each company in the group to repay all loans and advances made or to be made to it by the bank, whether by way of loan or an overdraft facility, and it is also extended so as to include a guarantee by each group company of all loans and advances made or to be made to the other companies in the group and a mortgage or charge on the assets of each group company to secure its own obligations to the bank and the guarantees it has given in respect of the other group companies' obligations.

The advantage of such composite documents are that the terms of the guarantees, mortgages and charges given by the companies in the group are made uniform for all loans and advances made by the bank to any group company, and when a particular loan or advance is made to such a company, all that need be specially negotiated with the bank are the amount of the loan, the mode of repayment and the interest rate and commission to be paid. No guarantees or security for the particular loan or advance are required (apart from guarantees or security given by outsiders to the group) because group guarantees and security have already been given by the composite document.

Moreover, by registering the composite security given by all the group companies at the Companies Registry against each of them under the Companies Act 1985, ss.395 and 396, the bank may obtain priority for payment of the total amount owing to it out of its security over the assets of all the group companies when they go into liquidation or receivership, and the only claims which may have priority over the banks' global claim will be certain debts owing to third persons which by statute or otherwise are entitled to priority for payment out of assets subject to floating charges vested in the bank.

3. CONTRACTUAL MODIFICATION OF THE NORMAL RULES GOVERNING LOAN AGREEMENTS, GUARANTEES AND SECURITY

Loan agreements

(1) Cross-default provisions
Loan agreements made by a bank with different companies belonging to the same group usually contain a provision that an act or event of default by any of the companies under the loan agreement or agreements entered into by the bank with it shall be deemed to be an act or event of default by every other company in the group under the loan agreement or agreements made by it with the bank, including the company which is a party to the loan agreement containing that provision. The consequence of this provision is that even if one group company has not defaulted under its own loan agreement, it is deemed to have done so if another company belonging to the group defaults under its loan agreement with the bank. The group of companies is thereby treated as a single entity although in law it is not, and a default by any part of the entity is deemed to be a default by the whole of it. The bank will then act appropriately under the default provisions of each loan agreement according to its terms. If the agreement made with a group company which is in deemed, but not actual, default makes the whole of its indebtedness to the bank immediately due and payable on a default, the bank may sue it for that indebtedness without first giving notice demanding payment, but if the bank is merely empowered to call for payment of its outstanding indebtedness on an actual or deemed default (as is usually the case), the bank must first call for payment before it issues a writ.

A cross-default provision of the kind described above is unnecessary if the bank has entered into a single loan agreement with all the

81

companies in the group making them jointly and severally liable for advances made by the bank to any of them, and providing that on a default by any company under the agreement all the companies which are parties to it shall be in default. Similarly, a cross-default provision is unnecessary if each of the companies in the group has guaranteed the indebtedness of each other such company, and the guarantees all provide that a default by any company in the group shall make the indebtedness of the guarantor company to the bank immediately due and payable, or payable on demand by the bank, as well as the indebtedness of the company which is in actual default.

If a bank channels the loans and advances it makes to a group of companies through the parent company or a specially designated finance company of the group, and that company re-lends to the operating group companies to meet their needs, there is no need for any special provision in respect of group defaults, provided each of the group companies guarantees the obligations of the company which borrows from the bank, because an act or event of default under the loan agreement between that company and the bank will trigger the liability of each of the other companies under their respective guarantees.

(2) *Independence of group companies' obligations*

Another contractual provision which is usually inserted in loan agreements, guarantees and documents creating charges over group companies' assets in connection with bank financing of a group of companies is that the obligations and liabilities of each company to the bank and the charges over its assets created by it shall be treated as independent and unconditional; that such obligations, liabilities and charges shall not be affected by the invalidity, voidability, ineffectiveness or unenforceability of any of the obligations or liabilities of any other group company or of any charges created by such a company over its own assets; and that the failure of any group company to enter into any undertaking or commitment to the bank, or to give any guarantee or security to it, shall not discharge or affect the obligations or liabilities of any other group company toward the bank or any charges over its assets which it has given.

It is doubtful whether this provision is legally necessary, because the obligations and liabilities of a surety are not conditional on a co-surety also guaranteeing the principal debt, unless it is expressly agreed between the surety and the creditor that they shall be so conditional; the mere fact that the surety knows that another person is intended to join in the guarantee does not discharge the surety from liability to the creditor if that other person does not do so.[9] The same

---

[9] *Horne* v. *Ramsdale* (1842) 9 M. & W. 329; *Coyte* v. *Elphick* (1874) 22 W.R. 541; *Byblos Bank S.A.L.* v. *Al Khudhairy* [1987] B.C.L.C. 232.

reasoning would seem to apply if one person gives a mortgage or charge over his assets knowing that another person is also intended to give a security for the same debt. In practice banks always ensure that there are no express conditions attached to group companies' obligations under loan agreements and guarantees or to their agreements to charge their assets to secure group indebtedness, and so the provision expressing the independence and unconditionality of each of the group companies' commitments to the banks is not essential, and is inserted purely *ex abundanti cautela*.

Guarantees

It is normal banking practice to include certain protective provisions in guarantees given in connection with loans made to companies belonging to the same group. These provisions often also appear in guarantees of bank loans and advances where there is no group relationship, but they are particularly important in the context of loans to group companies where the object is, so far as possible, to put the bank in the same position as if the group were a single company owning all the assets of the group companies collectively. The purpose of these special provisions is to negative certain rules of equity which discharge a guarantor of a debt from liability to the creditor, or which enable the guarantor to compete with the creditor in pursuing a claim against the principal debtor or a co-surety. Such claims would diminish the assets of the principal debtor or guarantor which are available to satisfy the creditor's claims, a matter of importance to the creditor if both the debtor and the guarantor are insolvent.

(1) *Maintenance of group companies' liabilities as guarantors*
The first of the special provisions inserted in guarantees of bank loans to groups is that no agreement subsequently made between the lending bank and the borrowing company or any other group company which releases it from liability for the whole or any part of the amount payable under the loan agreement or guarantee entered into by it, or which modifies any of the terms of the loan agreement or guarantee, shall release any other group company from its obligations under the guarantee given by it, or affect its obligations to the lending bank in any way. Often this provision is extended to include not only releases and modifications of the obligations of any of the group companies, but also acts of indulgence, waivers and extensions of time for the fulfilment of any group company's obligations, and also to compromises or arrangements consented to by the bank in respect of any group company.
Were it not for such a special provision, any agreement made between the lending bank and the group company which borrows from it, or any group company which guarantees the loan, would

operate to discharge all the guarantor companies' obligations to the bank if the agreement materially affected the borrowing or original guarantor company's obligations so as to increase the risk borne by the other group companies as sureties.[10] The independence and unaltered character of each guarantor company's obligations under the special provision in the guarantee is usually reinforced by a declaration in the guarantee that each guarantor company shall as between itself and the bank be deemed a principal debtor, and not merely a surety in respect of the obligations of the borrowing company.

(2) *Deferment of indemnity and contribution claims*
The other special provision usually inserted in guarantees of loans to group companies is designed to prevent a guarantor company competing with the bank in claiming an indemnity from the borrowing company or a contribution from a co-surety when the guarantor company has satisfied the whole or part of the borrowing company's indebtedness to the bank.

If a guarantor company has guaranteed the whole of the borrowing company's debt to the bank, it is entitled in equity to be indemnified or reimbursed by the borrowing company for all amounts it pays to the lending bank. There is no conflict of interest with the lending bank here if the borrowing company is insolvent but the guarantor company is solvent, because the bank will be paid in full by the guarantor company, and that company will then receive a dividend in the borrowing company's liquidation in respect of its indemnity claim. If the guarantor company has guaranteed the whole of the borrowing company's debt but has paid the bank only part of it (*e.g.* because it is itself insolvent), it cannot claim an indemnity for what it has paid in the liquidation of the borrowing company; this is because of the insolvency rule which prohibits two proofs being made in respect of the same debt of the borrowing company.[11] However, if the guarantor company has guaranteed only part of the borrowing company's indebtedness to the bank and has paid the bank in full in respect of that part, the guarantor company can prove for an indemnity in the liquidation of the borrowing company, even though this will diminish the assets of the borrowing company which are available to pay its remaining indebtedness to the bank (*i.e.* the guarantor and the bank will both receive the same smaller dividend in the pound on their respective claims).[12]

---

[10] *Clarke* v. *Henty* (1838) 3 Y. & C. Ex. 187; *Vyner* v. *Hopkins* (1846) 6 Jur. 889; *Oriental Financial Corp.* v. *Overend, Gurney & Co* (1871) 7 Ch.App. 142.
[11] *Re Oriental Commercial Bank, Ex p. European Bank* (1871) 7 Ch.App. 99; *Re Fenton, Ex p. Fenton Textile Association Ltd.* [1931] 1 Ch. 85.
[12] *Re Sass, Ex p. National Provincial Bank of England Ltd.* [1896] 2 Q.B. 12.

Under a separate rule of equity a surety is entitled to contribution from a co-surety if he has paid more than his proper share of the debt owed by the principal debtor,[13] and even if the surety has paid less than his proper share or has paid nothing at all, he can obtain an order directing his co-surety to pay the co-surety's proper share of the debt to the creditor so as to relieve the first surety from liability.[14] If the co-surety is insolvent, the creditor can prove against his assets for the whole amount the co-surety has guaranteed and which has not yet been paid by the debtor or any of the sureties; the first surety can at the same time prove against the co-surety's assets for the excess over his proper share of the total debt which the first surety has himself paid to the creditor. The consequence of this is that the total amount proved for against the co-surety's assets by the creditor and the first surety together is greater than if the creditor alone could prove, and the creditor therefore receives a smaller dividend in the pound.

The equitable rights of a guarantor to an indemnity from the principal debtor and to contribution from his co-sureties can be waived by him, and if he represents to the creditor before the principal debtor's indebtedness is incurred that the guarantor will not assert those rights in a way which may prevent the creditor recovering the whole or as much as possible of the debtor's indebtedness to the creditor, the guarantor will be estopped from doing anything which has that effect.[15] In practice banks are not content with a guarantor merely estopping himself by representation from asserting his rights to an indemnity or to contributions from his co-sureties, however, and they require him to agree expressly to renounce those rights. Where the guarantors are companies belonging to the same group as the borrowing company, the lending bank will therefore require the document or documents containing the guarantees to provide that as between each guarantor company and the bank, the guarantor company agrees to renounce any claim it may have at law or in equity or by any agreement to an indemnity for any payment it makes or for liability it incurs under the guarantee, and also to renounce any claim which the guarantor company may have to any contribution by any other person toward the amount of such a liability or payment. Furthermore, the guarantee will provide that if the guarantor company does receive any sum or valuable thing by way of an indemnity or contribution, or in full or partial satisfaction of any claim by it to an indemnity or contribution, it shall hold that sum or valuable thing in trust for the bank and shall transfer it to the bank on demand.

---

[13] *Davies* v. *Humphreys* (1840) 6 M. & W. 153; *Stirling* v. *Burdett* [1911] 2 Ch. 418.
[14] *Wolmerhausen* v. *Gullick* [1893] 2 Ch. 514.
[15] *Blake* v. *Gale* (1886) 32 Ch.D. 571; *Re Wickham* (1917) 34 T.L.R. 158.

Mortgages and charges

In general, no special provisions need be included in documents creating mortgages or charges over the assets of companies belonging to the same group merely because one or more of them are borrowing companies and others are guarantors. The lending bank should, of course, ensure that the arrangements it makes with the companies in the group cannot be attacked as an abuse of the powers of the directors of any of the companies involved, or at least, that the bank has no notice of facts which could support such an attack. The bank should also ensure that the group companies which guarantee loans or advances made to other group companies, or which mortgage or charge their own assets to secure such loans or advances, have power to do so by the express provisions of their respective memoranda of association, because a power to guarantee or secure the debts of third persons, even companies in the same group, will not be implied by law, except possibly where the company legitimately carries on a banking, insurance or cognate business.[16]

These matters, however, do not relate to the contents of the documents by which group companies create mortgages or charges. Such charges take effect in exactly the same way, whether the companies which create them are borrowing companies or guarantors, and the powers of realisation of the bank on a default are not affected by the capacities in which the companies give charges over their respective assets. The one special provision which should be included in mortgages or charges given by companies belonging to a group, however, is designed to combat the decision of Millett J. in a recent case that a bank cannot take a valid charge over the credit balance of an account held by the charging company with the bank, or over any debt which the bank owes to the company. The decision also calls for the appropriate modification of charges given by individual companies, but the problem is more acute when charges are given for the same loan by several companies, all or many of which have accounts with the lending bank.

(1) *Charges over debts owed by the chargee to the chargor*

The case in question, *Re Charge Card Services Ltd.*[17] was primarily concerned with the question whether the holder of a credit card issued by a bank or other credit institution is discharged from liability to pay for goods or services he obtains by the use of the card when he signs the voucher which the supplier will use to obtain reimbursement from the bank which issued the card, or whether the cardholder remains liable to pay the price to the supplier if the bank

[16] *Colman* v. *Eastern Counties Rly. Co.* (1846) 10 Beav. 1.
[17] [1987] Ch. 150.

fails to do so. Millett J. held that the credit card holder is not liable to pay the supplier on the bank or credit institution's default. He held additionally that if the credit institution which issues the credit card discounts and assigns its rights to reimbursement by the card-holders to a factoring company, which credits the institution with the discounted value of its rights against cardholders in an account with the institution, and the factor is contractually entitled to debit that account for amounts which it is unsuccessful in recovering from cardholders, the factor has no charge on the credit balance of the account with the institution, because such a charge would be upon a debt which the factor owes to the institution, and it is impossible for a debtor to have a security over a debt which he owes to the chargor. Instead, said Millett J., the factoring company has a right to set off or deduct amounts which cardholders are liable to pay, but which the factor is unable to recover from them, from the total discounted value of the amounts payable by all the cardholders which the factor has credited to the credit institution's account, and this is, of course, a purely personal right and not a charge on the credit balance of the account. In characterising the factor's right as one of set-off or deduction, Millett J. followed the view expressed by the House of Lords,[18] that a bank's right to consolidate a customer's accounts, some of which are in credit and others in debit, is simply a right of set-off, and does not give rise to a charge over the credit balances.

The significance of Millett J.'s decision, if it is correct, is that when a bank takes an express charge over the whole of the assets of a company, whether the company gives the charge as a borrower or as a guarantor of a loan made to another company, the charge will not extend to the credit balance of any account which the borrowing or guarantor company has with the bank, nor to any other indebted-ness of the bank to the company. Nevertheless, the bank will have the right to set off the borrowing company's debt to the bank against the company's credit balance when the company's debt becomes due and payable, provided that the credit balance is also due and payable or can be made so by the company demanding immediate repayment. A difficulty obviously arises if the credit balance is on a deposit account and is repayable only at a future date or on the giv-ing of so many months' notice, or if the deposit is represented by a certificate of deposit which will mature only at a future date. It is true that if the borrowing or guarantor company which is entitled to the deposit goes into liquidation, this element of futurity is no obstacle, and for the purpose of the liquidation the debt which the company owes to the bank can be set off immediately against the credit balance on the company's deposit account under the insol-vency set-off rules. But this is not so if the company is still a going

[18] *National Westminster Bank Ltd.* v. *Halesowen Presswork and Assemblies Ltd.* [1972] A.C. 785.

concern, or if it is in a receivership initiated by another secured creditor, and in that case only the ordinary rules of set-off will apply. In other words, if Millett J.'s ruling is correct, the bank would not be able to treat the credit balance on the company's deposit account as comprised in its charge over the company's assets, nor would it be able to exercise an immediate right of set-off, although it would be entitled to wait until the credit balance becomes repayable and set off the amount owed to it by the company against the credit balance at that time if the amount owed to it has not meanwhile been discharged.

(2) *Order of priorities*

An even greater danger for the bank if Millett J.'s decision is correct is that the borrowing company may validly charge the credit balance of any account it has with the lending bank with payment of debts it owes to its other creditors (*e.g.* to secure loans made to it after it has borrowed from or given a guarantee to the bank), and on giving notice of their charges to the lending bank, those other creditors would be entitled to payment out of the credit balance, subject only to the bank setting off debts due to it from the company which were immediately payable. Since the company's indebtedness to the bank as a borrower or guarantor would not be immediately due and payable unless the contractual repayment date had passed, or unless an event of default had occurred and had triggered an acceleration of the date for repayment, the lending bank would have no immediate right to repayment of the loan, and the company's creditors secured by charges on the company's credit balance with the lending bank would be entitled to recover the whole amount of the balance without deduction. It would not be possible to protect the bank in this situation by empowering it to close any account on which the company has a credit balance and to open a new account in its place, as it may do to preserve its priority when it has taken a charge over other property to secure the debit balance on a customer's current account.[19] Closing the company's account would not alter the facts that the lending bank's debt to the company is immediately due and payable and that the bank cannot exercise a right of set-off immediately. The bank has no immediate right to payment by the company because the company's indebtedness to it is not yet due, and, if Millett J. is correct, the bank cannot claim priority as a creditor with a prior charge on the account, because such a charge is not legally possible.

Banks are now seeking by contract to counter the effect of the ruling that they cannot have charges over the credit balances of accounts held with them by borrowers from the bank or by guaran-

---

[19] *Deeley* v. *Lloyds Bank Ltd.* [1912] A.C. 756.

tors of loans made by the bank. This is done by inserting in loan agreements and guarantees a contractual provision enabling the lending bank to set off against the principal of the loan made by the bank and against interest and charges accrued and accruing in respect of the loan, the total amount of credit balances on accounts held with the bank by the borrower or his guarantor, whether such balances are repayable on demand or only at a future date or on the giving of a length of notice. The extended contractual right of set-off enables the bank to treat the loan as though it were immediately repayable and available for set-off, and also to treat the credit balances on accounts held by the borrower or guarantor as though they, too, were immediately payable. This means that only the net balance of the indebtedness between the bank and the borrower or guarantor can be charged to the borrower or guarantor's other secured creditors, and whether the borrower or guarantor's indebtedness to the bank is greater than the credit balances on their accounts with the bank or not, the bank will effectively obtain priority over their other secured creditors. The fact that those creditors do not assent to this arrangement, or do not even know of it, would seem to make no difference. This is because the other creditors' security is over the borrowing or guarantor company's contractual rights against the bank, and if those rights are diminished by a contractual provision for set-off of this extended character, their security is correspondingly limited.

(3) *Group borrowing*

An extended provision for set-off by the bank is particularly necessary when a group company borrows from a bank with the support of guarantees given by other group companies. In that situation in order to make the bank's protection complete so that it may treat the group of companies as a single entity and the group's indebtedness as a single amount, the bank's contractual right of set-off should be extended further, so that whenever there are amounts which are owing, or which may at any time or on the occurrence of any contingency become owing, from the bank to any of the group companies, whether the borrowing company or a guarantor company, the bank may set off against such amounts the whole or any part of the amounts which are, or which may at any time or on any contingency become owing from any company in the group to the bank under the loan agreement or under any guarantee given in respect of it. Such a provision is, of course, effective against persons to whom a group company gives a charge over the credit balance of its accounts with a bank only if the company agrees to it before the charge is created or if the chargee agrees to the provision. It will not be binding on such a chargee if his charge over the credit balance of the bank account already exists when the provision is inserted in a loan agreement or guarantee entered into with the bank, and in that case the provision will become binding on the chargee only if he assents to it.

Subordination provisions

If a company has already borrowed on the security of its assets before it borrows from a bank, or in the case of a group company, before it guarantees a bank loan made to another company or other companies in the same group, the bank may as a condition of making its loan require that securities held by other creditors of the company, whether existing or prospective, shall be subordinated to the charges over the company's assets given to the bank. This is a particularly vital matter when a bank finances companies belonging to a group, because the amount the bank advances will depend largely on the value of the assets of the group as a whole, and the bank will need an assurance that its claim against the various group companies will rank first for payment out of the assets of the borrowing and guarantor companies.

A bank obviously cannot compel the holders of existing mortgages and charges over a borrowing or guarantor company's assets to agree to subordinate or postpone their charges to those now being given to the bank when the bank loan is negotiated, and the bank cannot achieve this by any unilateral act on its part. The priorities between competing mortgages or charges over the same assets are governed by the general law, and can only be varied by agreement between the interested parties. With regard to mortgages or charges created by the borrowing company after it has given security to the bank, the bank will normally have priority for its mortgage or charge anyway if it has perfected it and, where necessary, registered it at the Companies Registry under the Companies Act 1985, ss.395 and 396. The bank will be at risk of losing priority to the holders of charges created after its own only when it has taken a floating charge, and the company later creates a fixed or specific charge over assets which are comprised in the bank's floating charge, but even here the bank can protect itself to a considerable extent by imposing a contractual prohibition on the company creating such later mortgages or charges ranking in priority to the bank's charge.

(1) *Subordination of existing charges*

The legal problem which arises when a bank refuses to lend to a borrowing company because existing or future mortgages or charges created by it or by a company which guarantees the loan may rank in priority to the charges taken by the bank, is not in obtaining the assent of prior ranking chargees to subordinate their charges to the bank's charges, but in expressing that assent in a way which is legally binding on the prior ranking chargees. If their charges already exist, they may estop themselves from asserting the priority given to them by law by inducing the bank to make its advances to the borrowing company on the understanding the chargees will not claim priority for their charges. Here again, however, banks prefer to rely on explicit, documented agreements rather than conduct giving rise to estoppel, and so a bank will usually require the existing mortgagees or chargees to renounce their rights to priority over the bank's charges in the loan agreement with the borrowing company, or by a separate document. The renunciation will be given in consideration of the bank agreeing to make a loan or advances to the company, or the document containing the renunciation will be executed as a deed by the existing chargees so as to be binding on them even if no consideration is given to them. All that is necessary in equity to give the bank priority for its charge over the borrowing or guarantor company's assets is a legally binding contract by the renouncing mortgagees or chargees to give up their priority rights in favour of the bank, and it is not necessary for them to transfer their mortgages or charges to the bank or to declare themselves trustees of those mortgages or charges for the bank.

(2) *Anticipatory subordination*

The other legal difficulty in obtaining effective subordination agreements is where they are needed before the loan agreement is entered into between the borrowing company and the bank, or before another company in the same group gives a charge over its assets to secure the loan which is to be made by the bank. The legal problem is whether it is possible for the holders of mortgages or charges over a company's assets to give anticipatory renunciations of their rights to priority so as to enable the company to negotiate a secured loan with any bank in the future (subject to any agreed limitations), or so as to enable the company to give a charge over its assets to such a bank to secure a loan made to another company in the same group. The anticipatory renunciation of priority rights will be contained in a contract with the borrowing or guarantor company, and not with the bank which eventually makes a loan. It is most likely to be given by existing chargees who have an interest in the company as directors or shareholders, and are therefore willing to subordinate their priority rights so as to enable the company to negotiate a loan in the future on terms which the lending bank will find acceptable. The value of the anticipatory renunciation, if it can be made binding and irrevocable, is that it will enable the company to confer priority on the bank which eventually makes a loan to, or takes security from, the company, even though the persons who gave the anticipatory renunciation purport to revoke or rescind it, and even though they have ceased to have any interest in the company as directors, shareholders or otherwise.

There is no English decision where it has been held specifically that an anticipatory renunciation of priority rights by a mortgagee

91

or chargee is binding on a subsequent chargee who acts on the assumption that the renunciation will be effective, and that he will thereby acquire priority for his charge. There is, however, a decision of the Supreme Court of New Zealand (Adams J.) that in these circumstances the earlier mortgagee or chargee is estopped from asserting the right to priority which the law would otherwise give him, and his mortgage is therefore effectively postponed to the later charge.[20] In the United States the courts have frequently been called on to pronounce on the effectiveness of anticipatory renunciations of priority rights and subordination arrangements, and have held them to be binding on the earlier mortgagee or chargee who renounces his right to priority either:

(a) as a valid unilateral contract binding on him without any need for the later chargee to show that he relied on the anticipatory renunciation,[21] or

(b) as creating an equitable estoppel binding on the earlier mortgagee or chargee in favour of a later chargee who acts on it by making secured advances[22]; or

(c) as an implied assignment of, or charge on, the earlier mortgage or charge in favour of the later chargee, entitling him to payment first out of the proceeds of realising the earlier mortgage or charge[23]; or

(d) as giving rise to a constructive trust of the amount secured by the earlier mortgage or charge in favour of the later chargee.[24]

When the question of the effectiveness of an anticipatory renunciation of priority comes to be decided by the English courts, it may well be held that the renunciation is effective by way of an estoppel binding on the earlier mortgagee or chargee, but it is very doubtful whether any of the other reasons given by the American courts for treating the renunciation as binding will be adopted. On the other hand, the court could uphold the renunciation on an entirely new ground, namely, that the anticipatory renunciation immediately authorises the company to negotiate the subordination of the earlier mortgage or charge as a term of the contract it makes with the later chargee, and that this authority is irrevocable because of the company's obvious financial interest in exercising it. Reasoning along these lines would be amply supported by English decisions on the

[20] *Re Walker Construction Co. Ltd.* [1960] N.Z.L.R. 523.

[21] *Re A.B. Kreuger and Toll* (1938) 96 F. 2d 768; *Re Credit Industrial Corp.* (1966) 366 F. 2d 402.

[22] *Londner* v. *Perlman* 113 N.Y.S. 420; *Re Empire Granite Co.* (1942) 42 F.Supp. 440.

[23] *Re George P. Schinzel and Son Inc.* (1926) 16 F. 2d 289; *Re Handy-Andy Community Stores Inc.* (1932) 2 F.Supp. 97; *Bird and Sons Sale Corp.* v. *Tobin* (1935) 78 F.2d 371.

[24] *Re Dodge Freeman Poultry Co.* (1956) 148 F.Supp. 647.

irrevocability of authorities given for value to agents who have an interest in exercising the authority.[25]

(3) *Subordination in group situations*

The problem of ensuring that existing mortgages and charges are effectively subordinated is not unique to situations where a group company borrows from a bank on security, with or without the creation of security over their assets by other companies in the group. If all the companies in the group charge their respective assets to the bank to secure the loan or advance made to one of their number, there is, of course, no problem in subordinating mortgages and charges held by any group company over the assets of any other group company, because the group company which holds the mortgage or charge will itself expressly charge it to the bank as part of its own assets.

Difficulties can arise, however, if some of the group companies do not charge their assets to the bank to secure borrowing by other companies in the group which have already charged their assets to the non-participating group companies, or if a group company has given an earlier mortgage or charge over its assets to another company which is not a member of the group at the time but later becomes a group company, for example, as the result of a takeover bid successfully made for it by the parent company of the group. The aim of the bank is to obtain, so far as possible, a prior-ranking security over all the assets of all the companies in the group for loans and advances made by it to any of them, so that effectively the whole of the group's assets are subject to a first charge to the bank for the whole of the group's liabilities to the bank. A general renunciation by all the group companies of any priority for mortgages or charges which they hold or may acquire over the assets of all other companies which are or may become group companies is essential to assure the bank that it will have universal priority.

4. THE ENFORCEMENT OF GROUP LIABILITIES

The remedies available to a bank which has financed companies belonging to the same group are in no way affected by the status of the companies as holding companies and subsidiaries. The bank may therefore bring an action to recover the amount advanced to, or guaranteed by, any of the group companies when it is due and payable, and the bank may join all or any of the group companies which are liable to it as defendants in the action. If a group company which is so liable has not been joined as a defendant, a defendant company

---

[25] *Gaussen* v. *Morton* (1830) 10 B. & C. 731; *Smart* v. *Sandars* (1848) 5 C.B. 895; *Re Hannan's Express Gold Mining and Development Co. Carmichael's Case* [1896] 2 Ch. 643.

may apply to the court for it to be added as a co-defendant so that judgment may be given against all the group companies which are liable, and so that appropriate indemnity or contribution orders may be made as between them.[26] Additionally, group companies which are defendants to the bank's action may have other group companies which are obliged to indemnify them or to make contributions toward satisfying the bank's claim added as third parties to the action for the purpose of enforcing their obligations to the original defendants.[27] The question of indemnity and contribution between the group companies is, of course, of no concern to the bank, and is usually adjusted internally within the group without litigation. It is only where one or more of the group companies which have or may have indemnity or contribution claims against other group companies have minority shareholders, or different minority shareholders from the other group companies, that judicial rulings on those claims may be necessary to protect the interests of the minority shareholders.

If the lending bank seeks to enforce its claims against group companies by having them wound up by the court, it will usually present separate petitions against each of the group companies which is indebted to it, or which is liable to it as a guarantor, but it has been held permissible to present a single petition against two or more companies which are members of the same group if the debts on which the petition is based are identical for all the respondent companies (e.g. a loan or advance to one group company which is guaranteed by the others).[28] Separate winding-up orders are made against the companies which the court decides should be put into liquidation, and the winding-up of the affairs of each such company is conducted separately. Consequently, the bank must prove separately in the liquidation of each of the group companies for the amount owed to it by that company as a borrower or guarantor, and since the other debts proved in the liquidations of the various group companies will be different, as will the ratios between the respective total assets of those companies and their respective total debts, the dividend in the pound paid to the bank by the liquidators of the different group companies will not be the same.

The bank has an advantage if it has taken guarantees from all or some of the group companies for loans or advances made to another or others of them. The bank may prove in each separate liquidation for the whole amount owed to it by the company in question, whether as borrower or guarantor, and the bank is not obliged to make any deduction for the value of its right to prove for the same

---

[26] R.S.C. Order 15, r. 6(2).

[27] R.S.C. Order 16, r. 1(1).

[28] *Re Chancery Lane Registrars Ltd.* (unreported) December 9, 1983, referred to in *Re A Company* [1984] B.C.L.C. 307.

debt in the liquidations of other companies in the group.[29] The bank should lodge proofs for all its claims with the liquidators of the group companies as quickly as possible, however, because if it receives a payment in respect of the amount owed to it jointly and severally by two or more group companies from any such company or its liquidator, the bank must deduct the amount it receives (*e.g.* the amount of the dividend paid to it in the liquidation of one group company) from the amount for which it subsequently proves in the liquidation of another group company which is liable for the same debt. The result of the rule that a creditor can prove for the whole unpaid amount of a debt owed to him by several companies in liquidation in each of the liquidations if he has received nothing from any of the companies before he lodges his proofs, is that a lending bank may cumulate the dividends it receives in the liquidations of the different group companies, and it may as a result recover a total percentage of its claim greater than other creditors of individual companies in the group.

A lending bank will prefer to realise any security it holds for loans or advances made by it to companies belonging to a group rather than initiate the liquidation of the group companies or to seek administration orders against them. The reasons for this are the same as when the bank holds security for a loan made to a single company. The powers of the bank to realise a mortgage or charge created by a group company for the indebtedness of itself and any other group company are exactly the same as if the company did not belong to a group, and if receivers are appointed by the bank to realise the assets of different group companies, the receiverships must be separately conducted. In the same way as there can be no group liquidation of a group of companies, treating their assets as a single fund and their liabilities as a global amount to be paid out of that fund, so there can be no group receivership, even though the receiver appointed for all the group companies is the same insolvency practitioner.

---

[29] *Midland Banking Co.* v. *Chambers* (1869) 4 Ch.App. 398; *Re Rees, Ex p. National Provincial Bank of England Ltd.* (1881) 17 Ch.D. 98.

V

Alternative Financing and Future Developments

The final Chapter of this book will be concerned with two matters, namely, the alternative ways in which companies can raise the finance they need without relying on loans or other financing facilities offered by the commercial banks, and secondly, the developments which are likely to take place in the financing arrangements which commercial banks will make in the foreseeable future.

The first of these matters involves an examination of what may be called non-banking financial facilities, and 20 years ago one could safely say that all the services which come under this heading well merited that description, because none of them were then provided by the commercial banks. With the enlargement of the kinds of transactions engaged in by commercial banks in more recent times, it is no longer true to say that all these facilities are outside those provided by the commercial banks or their specialised subsidiaries.

The subject matter of the first part of this Chapter will therefore consist in part of fringe banking services, which now provided by banks and their subsidiaries but also very substantially by institutions other than banks (such as finance companies, property companies and investment trusts), and in part of non-banking services which up to the present the commercial banks have not provided. The examination of this borderland of the services provided by the banks leads on naturally to an investigation of the additional services which commercial banks are likely to provide in the future. This is not merely fanciful speculation; the need for such services already exists, and tentative, experimental steps have already been taken toward providing them. The financial needs of companies in the future can be envisaged without difficulty; the fascinating question is how far and how quickly will the banks go toward satisfying them.

1. FINANCE FOR COMPANIES PARTLY PROVIDED BY BANKS

The ways of financing companies which are used by non-banking institutions, but also to a growing extent by the specialised subsidiaries of commercial banks, comprise forms of financing which are often grouped together under the rubrics of off-balance sheet financing and financing which involves the disposal of fixed assets by companies but the retention of their use. These forms of financing are very different in character and result. The forms which are labelled off-balance sheet financing enable a company to acquire assets it needs without an immediate outlay of capital and without borrowing, and they are called off-balance sheet financing because they do not immediately affect the contents of the company's balance sheet by adding assets which it acquires or by subtracting the cash value of those assets. The forms of financing which involve a disposal of assets of the company but the retention by it of their use do, on the other hand, affect the company's balance sheet by diminishing the amount of assets shown as belonging to the company, but compensate for this diminution by increasing the company's cash resources.

Off-balance sheet financing

The simplest form of off-balance sheet financing is hiring or leasing, that is, a transaction by which the company acquires the right to possess or use assets which it requires for an agreed period in return for a periodic payment called a rent, rental or hiring charge. The subject matter of the transaction may be land and buildings or moveable plant and equipment.

(1) *Leases of land and buildings*

If the subject matter of a lease is land and buildings, the financial institution which finances the transaction acquires the freehold or a long leasehold in the land and buildings from a third person, and it then grants a lease of the property to the company at a full commercial rent without payment of a premium. The company thereby acquires the right to the possession and use of the property for the duration of the lease granted to it, and its obligations (*e.g.* to keep the property in repair, to insure it, to use it only for the purpose of the company's business undertaking) are negotiated with the financial institution and embodied in a formal lease. The institution is rarely a bank or subsidiary of a bank, but is usually an insurance company, a property investment company, a property development company or, occasionally, an investment trust company. The company, as a business tenant, is protected by the provisions of Part II of the Landlord and Tenant Act 1954, which enable it to obtain a renewal of the lease on its expiration, or alternatively, compensation for disturbance if the lease is not renewed, and the company is also protected by the Landlord and Tenant Act 1927 (as amended) which entitles the company to compensation for improvements it makes to the property during the lease. The advantage to the company of taking a lease at a commercial rent of property where it carries on its business undertaking rather than purchasing the property or taking a lease in consideration of a premium and a lower rent, is that the company does not need to make a capital outlay when the lease is granted, but instead the full rent it agrees to pay becomes part of the expenses of carrying on its business undertaking, and will, if the company is trading profitably, be fully discharged, like its other overheads, out of its gross revenue or turnover. Moreover, the rent paid by the company will be deductible in calculating its profits for the purpose of corporation tax.

(2) Leases and hiring agreements in respect of equipment

Leases or hiring agreements in respect of plant or equipment may be of two kinds, namely, simple hiring agreements under which the company pays the economic value of the use it makes of the equipment as a rental or hiring charge, and finance leases which are of a sufficient duration for the total rental paid by the company to yield to the owner of the equipment the initial cost of the equipment with interest and to reimburse the owner for the expenses of maintaining the equipment which are borne by him. In legal form the two kinds of leases are similar; the company is entitled by them to the exclusive possession and use of the equipment as a bailee in return for a periodic rental or hiring charge, and either the company or the owner of the equipment agrees to maintain it during the lease (the cost of doing so being reflected in the level of the rental or hiring charge). At the expiration of the lease or hiring the company is required to return the equipment to the owner in a stipulated condition, having regard to whichever of them bears the cost of maintaining it. Often the company is given an option to renew the lease or hiring on similar terms when it expires, and in some agreements the company also has an option to purchase the equipment at its then value or at an arithmetically calculated price.

The differences between the hiring agreements and finance leases are economic and commercial rather than legal. The owner of equipment which is hired for use by the company during a short period, or even an extended period, at a rental which reflects the current value of the use which can be made of the equipment is usually a plant hire company, or the manufacturer of the equipment or its plant hire subsidiary, and it is usual for the maintenance and repair of the equipment to be undertaken by the owner as a separate service which is charged for, or in consideration of an inclusive rental. The owner of the hired equipment carries on the business of hiring plant or equipment suitable for use in certain trades or industries (*e.g.* earth moving machinery in the building industry, computers for businesses which keep extensive financial records), and charges rentals which cover the cost of the equipment over its expected useful life and also the cost of maintaining, repairing and insuring the equipment plus a percentage mark up on the total of these costs so as to yield the level of profit which the owner requires.

(3) *Finance leases*

A finance lease, on the other hand, is a financing transaction dressed up in the form of a lease. The owner of the equipment is always a finance company which is either an independent concern or a subsidiary of a bank, and the equipment is purchased by the finance company from the manufacturer or a dealer so that it may be leased to the company which needs it. The lease is granted for a period closely related to the expected useful life of the equipment at a rental which over the period of the lease will cover the initial and current costs which the finance company incurs plus a rate of interest on those costs and a financing charge for undertaking the transaction. In finance leases the company which uses the equipment is often given the option of terminating the lease after a certain minimum period on paying a stipulated sum to compensate the finance company, and even more frequently, the company is given the option to continue the lease at a substantially reduced rent after the agreed period of the lease has expired. Where the company needs to renew the equipment after it has been in use for a period substantially less than its useful life, a finance lease may be employed under which a higher rent is charged than would be charged under a longer lease, but the rent is retrospectively reduced if the company takes a lease of replacement equipment from the same finance company, or alternatively, the rent for the replacement equipment is reduced to a level comparable to that which would be charged under a lease for the full economically useful life of the replacement equipment. Thus, by paying a somewhat higher net rental under both the initial and the replacement leases, the company can ensure that its equipment is always no older than is acceptable to it. This kind of arrangement is particularly prevalent in leases of computers.

There are a number of variations on the two basic kinds of hiring or leasing agreements for plant and machinery, particularly in respect of finance leases. A finance lease may contain an option for the lessee company to purchase the equipment either at the end of the lease at a price based on the residual value of the equipment, or during the lease at a price based on the discounted value of the unpaid instalments of rent which would become payable under the lease if it continued. In that case the lease becomes for legal and tax purposes a hire-purchase agreement, and merely contains a greater degree of flexibility than a conventional hire purchase agreement in that it enables the company to become the owner of the equipment at any time, and not only when it has paid all the rental instalments.

(4) *Hire purchase credit sale and conditional sale agreements*

If the company wishes to acquire the ownership of the equipment in any event but wishes to pay for it by instalments, it is more appropriate for it to enter into a conventional hire-purchase agreement with the finance company which acquires the equipment for it.

Alternatively, the company may purchase the equipment from the finance company either under a credit sale agreement by which the ownership of the equipment passes to the company immediately, subject to the right of the finance company to re-possess the equipment and thereby re-acquire the ownership of it if the company defaults in paying the instalments of the purchase price at the agreed times, or under a conditional sale agreement by which the passing of ownership of the equipment to the company is deferred until it has paid all the instalments of the purchase price.

Commercially and economically there is no difference between hire-purchase, credit sale and conditional sale agreements. The hire rental or the instalments of the purchase price are calculated in exactly the same way by dividing the total costs, interest and transaction charges payable to the finance company by the number of instalments to be paid, and the rights of the finance company to re-possess and dispose of the equipment if the company defaults are effectively the same. There is, however, the formal difference between hire-purchase and and conditional sale agreements on the one hand and credit sale agreements on the other, that the former are off-balance sheet transactions and the equipment appears as an asset in the company's accounts only when all the instalments have been paid to the finance company, whereas acquisitions under credit sales are not off-balance sheet, and equipment so acquired should appear in the company's balance sheet as an asset immediately on acquisition, but counterbalanced by a provision on the other side of the balance sheet for the amount of the unpaid instalments of the purchase price.

(5) *Tax considerations*

If plant or equipment is leased or hired to a company and used by it for the purpose of its business, the rental it pays to the owner is deductible from the company's gross revenue when calculating the amount of its profits on which it pays corporation tax. The finance company which owns the plant or equipment is, of course, taxable on the profit it obtains from rentals it receives under leases and hiring agreements entered into by it, but it is entitled to deduct from its annual profits for tax purposes a statutory capital allowance calculated at a percentage of the cost to it of the plant or equipment less the total of such allowances previously given.[1] On the other hand, a company which acquires plant or equipment under a credit sale agreement, or which will or may acquire the ownership of it under a hire-purchase or conditional sale agreement, is entitled to deduct from its annual profits for tax purposes the statutory capital allowance calculated at a certain percentage of the cash price of the plant

[1] Finance Act 1971, s.46(1).

or equipment when it entered into the agreement (*i.e.* the total of the instalments payable under the agreement other than interest and transaction charges) less capital allowances previously given.[2] The company is also entitled to deduct the annual interest element in the instalments it pays to the finance company in arriving at its taxable profits, but it is, of course, not entitled to deduct the instalments themselves. The result of this is that the company is treated for tax purposes as if it were the owner of the plant or equipment, even though it has not yet acquired ownership, but merely has the right to do so if it pays all the instalments under the hire purchase or conditional sale agreement.

Capital allowances are not now as important as they were in connection with the financing of the acquisition of plant and equipment by companies before March 1984, when 100 per cent. of the cost or cash price of the plant or equipment was deductible from the company's profits in the year when the equipment was leased to the company or delivered to it under a credit sale, conditional sale or hire purchase agreement. Leases of plant and equipment were at that time made to companies which could not use the capital allowance of 100 per cent. because their profits were insufficient, simply in order to enable the finance company which granted the lease to claim the allowance itself, and to deduct it from its own profits for tax purposes. The finance company then conceded a correspondingly reduced rent to the lessee company. Now that only annual percentage allowances can be deducted from the finance company's profits for tax purposes, the incentive for companies to take leases of equipment purely for fiscal reasons is less, but the incentive is still there to a reduced extent if the company would not be able to make full use of the annual allowances itself if it purchased the plant or equipment outright with borrowed money.

Disposals of assets

(1) *Sale and lease back*

It is obvious that a company which wishes to raise money to finance its business can do so by selling some of its assets, but if the assets are essential for it to continue carrying on its business as a going concern, the sale and disposal will defeat the very object it is intended to achieve. A compromise which enables the company to raise the money it needs, but at the same time to retain the use of the assets it disposes of, is for the company to sell the assets for a capital sum paid to it immediately and to take back a lease of the assets from the purchaser for a lengthy period at a commercial rent, which

---

[2] *Ibid.* s.44(1), (2) and (4) and s.45(1).

is calculated to take account of the fact that the purchaser will not only receive an income in the form of rent, but will also have a valuable reversion on the lease granted to the company.

Sale and lease-back transactions are primarily employed where a company owns the freehold or a long leasehold interest in land, and the purchasers who finance companies in this way are usually insurance companies, pension fund trustees, or land investment companies, and only rarely the specialised subsidiary companies formed by banks. Sale and lease-back transactions may also be entered into in respect of other assets owned by companies, such as plant and equipment, patent and other industrial property rights, mining and oil leases and exclusive trading or operational concessions obtained in overseas countries where the company has made direct investments. It would also be possible for a company to sell and take a lease back of its whole undertaking, as is sometimes done as a financing operation in France, Germany and Switzerland.

Up to the present in the United Kingdom sale and lease-back transactions have been entered only in respect of plant and equipment as well as land and buildings, and they have not been employed in respect of intangible property as a means of financing. When companies have sold their existing plant and equipment to finance companies and taken leases back, the sale price has always been fixed at somewhat less than the realisable value of the plant or equipment. The rental payable by the company under a lease-back is calculated in the same way as it is calculated under a finance lease so as to reimburse the finance company for the sale price with the addition of interest and a transaction charge, and for obvious reasons the duration of the lease has been limited to the remaining useful life of the plant or equipment. Sometimes the lease contains an option for the company to re-purchase the plant or equipment, or instead of a lease, the company enters into a conventional hire purchase, credit sale or conditional sale agreement with the finance company under which the company will re-acquire the ownership of the plant or machinery. Transactions of these kinds are always entered into by companies with finance companies and not with banks, but many such finance companies have in recent years been formed or acquired as subsidiaries by commercial banks, and so this form of financing is not entirely outside the banking sector.

(2) *Treatment of transactions as mortgages*

The dangers for an investment or finance company which purchases and leases back assets to a company as a means of providing it with needed cash resources, is that equity may treat the whole transaction as a mortgage. If this were done, the company would be able to re-acquire the assets on repaying the purchase price received by it plus interest and costs, even though it has no express contractual option to re-purchase, and equity would allow the company to exercise such a right of redemption at any time, even though the company has failed to pay the rent reserved by the terms of the lease. The consequence of this for the financing concern would be that it would not be able to enforce the terms of the sale and lease-back strictly, and it could be deprived of its reversion on the lease whenever the company chose to redeem, unless the court makes a foreclosure order on its application.

In transactions with private persons the court has sometimes treated a sale and lease back as a mortgage, whether an express option to repurchase was given to the seller or not,[3] but this has not been invariably so.[4] The decisions are difficult to distinguish, because the court has repeatedly emphasised that it is the intentions of the parties shown by the surrounding circumstances which determine the matter, and not the form of the agreement. In cases where the transaction was of a commercial character, as it always will be when the sale and lease-back is designed as a means of financing a company, the courts have been strongly inclined to treat the transaction as being what the parties have expressed it to be, and not as being a mortgage. There has in fact been only one case, where the purpose of the transaction was to provide the company with temporary financial accommodation, in which the court has treated a sale and lease-back to a company as though it were a mortgage.[5] In all other cases the court has treated sales and lease-back transactions with companies as taking effect literally, and this has been so whether the assets in question have been simply leased or hired back to the company,[6] whether the company was given an option to repurchase the assets,[7] or whether the company undertook that the finance company would receive a certain minimum return from the transaction.[8]

If a transaction is held by the court to be a sale and lease-back and not a mortgage, the court cannot give equitable relief from the termination of the company's rights under the lease or hiring, or from the strict enforcement of its obligations.[9] This is so even if the property leased back is land,[10] except where the transaction is designed to enable the company to pay the purchase price of land which it has

---

[3] *Re Duke of Marlborough's Estate* [1894] 2 Ch. 133; *Polsky* v. *S.A. Services Ltd.* [1951] 1 All E.R. 185.

[4] *Goodman* v. *Frierson* (1813) 2 Ball & B. 274; *Williams* v. *Owen* (1840) 5 My. & Cr. 303; *Hare* v. *Nicoll* [1966] 2 Q.B. 130.

[5] *Grangeside Properties Ltd.* v. *Collingwood Securities Ltd.* [1964] 1 All E.R. 143.

[6] *Yorkshire Rly Waggon Co.* v. *McClure* (1881) 19 Ch.D. 478, affirmed (1882) 21 Ch.D. 309.

[7] *Stoneleigh Finance Ltd.* v. *Phillips* [1965] 2 Q.B. 537.

[8] *Re George Inglefield Ltd.* [1933] Ch. 1.

[9] *Leeman* v. *Yorkshire Rly Waggon Co.* (1881) 50 L.J. Ch. 293; *Cramer* v. *Giles* (1883) Cab & El. 151; *Hare* v. *Nicoll* [1966] 2 Q.B. 130.

[10] *Pegg* v. *Wisden* (1856) 16 Beav. 239.

acquired immediately before the sale and lease-back.[11] A company which has taken a lease-back of land can, of course, seek relief by the court from the forfeiture of its lease under the Common Law Procedure Act 1852, ss.210 to 212 in respect of non-payment of rent, and under the Law of Property Act 1925, s.146 in respect of breaches of its other obligations, but there are no similar statutory provisions for relief when the lease-back relates to assets other than land.

(3) *Tax considerations*

The tax consequences of lease-backs are the same as those of leasing, hiring, hire purchase, credit sale and conditional sale transactions, where the company in question has not previously owned the assets comprised in the lease-back. Nevertheless, the parties to a sale and lease-back should ensure that the price paid to the company for the sale of the assets to the financing concern represents their real, saleable value, and that the price is not artificially diminished in return for a corresponding reduction in the rent payable by the company under the lease back. If this is done the company may be taxable on the difference between the realisable value of the assets and the price actually paid to it for them as a capital gain arising on a sale at an undervalue.[12]

Conversely, a lease-back of an asset to a company should not reserve a rent to the financing concern which exceeds a reasonable commercial rent, having regard to the nature and condition of the assets leased back. If the lease-back is of land, the company may not deduct from its gross revenue as a deductible expense for tax purposes more than the amount of a commercial rent, and the excess rent it pays is disallowed.[13] The same rule applies when a lease-back is taken by the company of assets other than land; the amount of a commercial rent for such assets is taken to be the rent which might be expected to be paid under a lease granted at current market values at the date of the lease-back if the lease were granted for the remainder of the anticipated normal working life of the assets and the rent were payable at a uniform rate.[14]

2. ISSUES OF SHARES AND DEBENTURES

Introductory

Traditionally the resources of a company with which it establishes and expands its business should be the share capital it issues on its formation and when it later appeals again to its existing shareholders or investors generally for further permanent funds. To this

---

[11] *Re Dagenham (Thames) Docks Co, ex p. Hulse* (1873) 8 Ch.App. 1022; *Kelmer* v. *British Columbia Orchard Lands Ltd.* [1913] A.C. 319.

[12] Capital Gains Tax Act 1979, s.29A(1).

[13] Income and Corporation Taxes Act 1970, s.491(1) and (4).

[14] *Ibid.* s.493(1), (2) and (6).

capital must be added the profits which the company earns but does not distribute as dividends to its shareholders. Such profits or revenue reserves are often capitalised so as to prevent them permanently from being distributed as dividends, and bonus shares equal to the capitalisation are then issued to the existing equity shareholders of the company in proportion to their existing holdings.

This scenario was, of course, the 19th century ideal, when the accepted view was that companies should expand by internal growth and by ploughing back into their undertakings a substantial part of their profits, and that borrowing should be resorted to only to finance current trading operations so as to bridge the gap between the time when the company incurred expenses to manufacture or acquire the products which it marketed and the time when it received the proceeds of marketing them. The traditional ideal was not wholly accurate even if the 19th century, and prosperous and expanding companies, as well as static ones, at that time often found it necessary to issue debentures or later, debenture stock, in order to raise loans for substantial periods to supplement the amounts they raised by issuing shares. Because of this need to raise loan capital as well as share capital, the duration of debenture loans increased progressively in the second half of the 19th century. By the beginning of this century it was not uncommon for medium sized and large companies to have issued debentures with a life of 20 or 25 years, and for such long term borrowing to account for up to a third of the total share and loan capital raised by the company.

The traditional picture of a company relying on its share capital and capitalised profits alone, even if it was true at any time, has long ceased to represent the way companies are financed. During the last 40 years, despite successive but relatively short periods when market conditions have been favourable to capital raising, companies have increasingly relied on finance provided by banks and their specialised subsidiaries to provide the cash resources they need. The most remarkable phenomenon to be observed during the last 15 years is the multiplication of the ways in which bank finance has been provided for companies. During the years of economic recession beginning in the mid 1970s, which have been followed by only a hesitant economic revival in the 1980s, accelerating noticeably only during the last three years, large scale issues of equity shares by medium-sized and large companies have been at a substantially lower level than normal, and debenture issues to the investing public at large have been almost non-existent. The slack has been taken up by the varied forms of bank financing, ranging from overdrafts to medium-term and long-term loans and to the many other financing devices which we have considered in this book. Bank finance has largely superseded the raising of capital by the traditional methods. Nevertheless, share and debenture issues remain an important method for companies to raise medium and long term capital, and because the revival of the new issue market now seems well on the way, a brief examination of the ways in which finance may be raised on the new issue market is not out of place here.

At present the commercial banks take only a minor part in the raising of capital by large and medium sized companies making new issues of shares and debentures. This has been through the activities of the merchant banking subsidiaries which the commercial banks have formed or acquired over the last 15 or so years. No doubt the banks would have enlarged their share of this business more substantially if the new issue market had been more active during those years, and it is certain that they will have a larger role in this field when the current national economic revival has fully developed. In the meantime the services needed in connection with the new issue of securities on a large scale are provided predominantly by the 80 or so merchant banks and issuing houses which specialise in this work. Smaller companies whose shares and debentures are not listed on the Stock Exchange or admitted to dealing on the Unlisted Securities Market of the Stock Exchange or on the so-called Third Market established by the Stock Exchange in January 1987, rarely make issues of shares or debentures after their initial issue, but the occasions when such companies need to do so (*e.g.* on the acquisition of other companies and on management buy-outs) are increasing. A market is made in the shares and other securities of certain such companies by some 10 of the largest dealing firms which are licensed to deal in securities and which make up the Over the Counter Market, and these firms also attend to new issues of securities for cash and capitalisation issues made by such companies. Some of this work has also been undertaken by the merchant banking subsidiaries of the commercial banks, but the long established merchant banks tend to intervene only when companies are ready to seek a Stock Exchange listing or an admission to the U.S.M. Probably the recent establishment by the Stock Exchange of the less formal Third Market to provide for dealings in the shares and debentures of smaller companies in parallel to the Over the Counter Market will bring the long established merchant banks, as well as the merchant banking subsidiaries of the commercial banks, into the area of new issue business for smaller companies.

Security issues by large and medium-sized public companies

A company which has a Stock Exchange listing for its shares, or at least has its shares admitted to the Unlisted Securities Market of the Stock Exchange, will usually be a large or medium-sized concern, and the total value or market capitalisation of its shares will necessarily be at least £5m. Such a company may raise further share capital in any one of three ways, namely, firstly, by making a rights issue to its existing equity shareholders, that is, all its shareholders other than the holders of preference shares carrying a fixed annual preferential dividend and the right to repayment of capital in the company's liquidation in priority to its ordinary shareholders, but no other rights to participate in the company's assets or profits; or secondly, by issuing the new shares to a merchant bank or issuing house or making the shares available to investors through a firm of sponsoring broker/dealers so that the merchant bank, issuing house or firm or broker/dealers may place the shares with its clients (mainly institutional investors) and also place a percentage of them with the investing public, who will acquire the shares through the market; or thirdly, by making a public offer of the shares by means of a prospectus or listing particulars advertised in the national press and inviting the investing public to apply for the shares at a fixed issue price either from the company, or from a merchant bank or issuing house which has agreed to subscribe for the shares so as to offer them for sale to the public.

Offers of convertible debentures (that is, debentures carrying an option for the holder to convert them into fully paid shares) and debentures with subscription warrants attached (that is, debentures carrying the right for the holder to subscribe for a number of shares proportionate to his holding of debentures) are made in the same way, but offers of debentures which carry no conversion or subscription rights are always made either by an offer for subscription or sale which is open to the investing public as a whole, or by a private placing of the debentures by negotiation with an institutional investor or a syndicate of such investors.

(1) *Rights offers*

Both the Companies Act 1985, and the Stock Exchange Rules require issues for cash of equity shares and securities convertible into equity shares to be made primarily to the existing equity shareholders of the company in proportion to their existing holdings, but under the Companies Act a general meeting of the company can waive this requirement by passing a special resolution to that effect,[15] and the Stock Exchange may permit issues of equity shares for cash by other methods in exceptional circumstances, including a waiver of existing shareholders' preferential subscription rights by a special resolution passed by a general meeting of the company. A proportionate offer of shares for cash subscription made in this way is a rights offer, and it is made by the company or an issuing house which has agreed to subscribe for the shares subject to the existing shareholders' subscription rights, issuing provisional letters of allotment to all the company's equity shareholders informing them of their subscription rights, and that in anticipation that they will exercise such rights, there has been allotted to each of them a

[15] Companies Act 1985, s.89(1) to (4) and s.95(1) and (2).

107

proportionate number of the new shares. The shareholder may then either accept the shares allotted to him and pay the fraction of the issue price which is payable on allotment, or may do this and then sell the shares as partly paid by renouncing or assigning his rights to them to a purchaser, or he may sell the shares as nil paid to such a purchaser and leave it to him to pay the whole amount of the issue price payable on allotment and later.

When the whole issue price of the shares has been paid by the original recipients of the provisional letters of allotment or their renouncees, the letters of allotment are surrendered by their then holders to the company, which registers them as members of the company in its register of members and issues fully paid share certificates to them. Issues of bonus shares paid for by capitalising part of the company's profits or reserves are made in the same way, but of course no issue price is payable by the shareholders, who receive the provisional letters of allotment for the shares credited as fully paid. The shareholders are free to sell and renounce their rights to the bonus shares to whomsoever they choose.

(2) *Placings*

Placings on the Stock Exchange of equity shares or securities convertible into equity shares by a previously unlisted company can only be made if the expected market value of the securities does not exceed £15m., if the company seeks a Stock Exchange listing for its shares, or £5m. if it seeks a quotation of the securities on the Unlisted Securities Market. There is no limit on the value of securities which may be placed by a company which already has a Stock Exchange listing or whose securities are already dealt in on the Unlisted Securities Market.

When equity shares or securities with a market value exceeding £2m. are placed on the Stock Exchange on behalf of a company which does not already have a listing or quotation for its securities, the merchant bank, issuing house or firm of sponsoring broker/dealers which handles the placing must make at least 25 per cent. of the securities available on the market, that is, available for acquisition by the investing public generally either by them being offered to the public by a prospectus, or by them being taken by one or more independent market makers who will sell them on the Stock Exchange, or by an independent firm of broker/dealers taking the securities for distribution to its own clients or for re-sale on the market. This means that the institution which carries out the placing can place up to 75 per cent. of the securities with its own clients, which may include some, but not all, of the institutional investors who wish to acquire holdings of the securities. To ensure that the marketing arrangements are reasonable and that a false market will not be made in the securities, a marketing statement showing the proposed division of the securities between the merchant bank, issuing house or firm of sponsoring broker/dealers and their respective clients and the market must be delivered to the Stock Exchange with the formal application for the admission of the securities to listing or to dealing on the Unlisted Securities Market, as the case may be. Placings of securities are usually underwritten if substantial in amount, and when a firm of sponsoring broker/dealers is employed by a company to place securities, the issuing company always underwrites the issue, because the firm of broker/dealers does not commit itself to subscribe for the securities or to find subscribers for them in any event.

(3) *Public offers*

Shares and debentures which are comprised in a public offer are offered to the investing public at large by a prospectus or listing particulars which specify the issue price and the instalments by which it is to be paid, and also in the case of an offer for sale of securities, the net proceeds of the issue which will be paid to the company (thus revealing the "turn" or difference between this sum and the total issue price which the merchant bank or issuing bank will receive) together with a considerable amount of statutory and other information about the company. The prospectus or listing particulars include an application form by means of which any member of the investing public may apply to the company (if it makes a direct offer to the public) or to the merchant bank or issuing house (if it offers to sell securities for which it has agreed to subscribe) for the number of shares or the amount of debentures he wants.

If the offer is oversubscribed, the company, merchant bank or issuing house devises and publishes a scheme of allotment by which applications are scaled down, so that the available shares or debentures will be allotted without the company issuing any excess shares or debentures. There is no obligation to scale down applications proportionately, and usually the scheme involves the total elimination of very small applications (which involve a disproportionate amount of administrative work) and the allotment of progressively smaller percentages of the successive bands of larger amounts of securities applied for. If the offer of shares or debentures is under-subscribed, the balance of securities offered but not taken up by the public are subscribed for by the merchant bank or issuing house, or if the issue had been underwritten, by the underwriters at the same issue price as subscribers under the listing particulars. They then sell the securities on the market over a period of time so as to recover their outlay without depressing the current dealing price of the securities excessively.

(4) *The Over-the-Counter Market*

Issues of shares or debentures by licensed dealers in the Over-the-Counter Market are usually made by placing them with institutional

109

and other investors, but a few issues have been made by means of offers to the public inviting subscriptions or by offers for sale, both of which involve the issue of prospectuses. Rights offers of equity shares are also sometimes made through licensed dealers. Whatever method of issuing securities is employed when a licensed dealer acts as an intermediary for the issuing company, it is only when the issue is managed by one of the larger licensed dealers that it will also undertake to make a market in the securities after they have been issued, and so provide the means by which an investor who holds the securities may dispose of them. It is likely that companies which hitherto have marketed their securities through licensed dealers on the Over-the-Counter Market will increasingly market them instead on the Third Market of the Stock Exchange.

(5) *The role of the banks in marketing securities*

The participation of the commercial banks in the issue of securities by large and medium-sized companies is normally confined to the administrative work involved in receiving and processing applications for the securities from investors and to receiving and accounting for amounts paid by them on application and allotment and the later instalments of the issue price. Nevertheless, the merchant banking subsidiaries of the commercial banks play as full a part in the placing of securities and the offering of securities to the investing public for subscription or sale as do the independent merchant banks. The share of new issue work which they have undertaken has grown considerably in recent years, and is likely to continue growing in the future.

Security issues by smaller companies

Smaller companies which are not eligible for a Stock Exchange listing for their equity shares because their market capitalisation would be too small, and companies whose size or needs for additional capital do not justify an application for their securities to be admitted to dealing on the Unlisted Securities Market of the Stock Exchange, may if they are public companies, seek the assistance of a licensed dealer to introduce their securities on the Over-the-Counter market. Many smaller companies hav been encouraged to do this because of the personal tax concessions made to new subscribers for shares in such companies under the Business Expansion Scheme introduced by the Finance Act 1983 s.26, as a successor to the Business Start-Up Scheme, which was initiated in 1981. For investors to obtain these personal tax advantages the company and its shareholders must satisfy certain conditions, including the requirement that the company must have no part of its share or loan capital listed on the Stock Exchange or admitted to dealings on the Unlisted Securities Market. In fact, the growth of the Over-the-

Counter Market during the last five years has been mainly attributable to the use made by companies of the Business Expansion Scheme as a means of raising fresh capital.

In addition to the public companies whose shares are not dealt in on the Stock Exchange or on the Over-the-Counter Market, there are some public companies which have not sought to raise capital through any market. There are also the numerous private companies, which are prohibited by the Companies Act 1985, s.81(1) from offering their shares or debentures for subscription by the public or any section of it, and from having their securities offered for sale by an issuing house or other intermediary which agrees with the company to subscribe for the securities with a view to offering them for sale to the public. The result of these restrictions is that private companies can only raise capital by private negotiations with individual or corporate investors, or by making offers to their existing shareholders or debenture holders, or to employees of the company or to members of the families of shareholders or employees.

Moreover, unless the company's memorandum or articles of association otherwise provide or a special resolution to the contrary is passed by a general meeting of the company, it must offer new equity shares or securities which are to be paid for in cash for subscription proportionately by its existing equity shareholders before allotting them in any other way.[16] When a private company does make an offer of its shares or debentures to its shareholders or debenture holders or to its employees, therefore, the offer must either be unrenounceable and so unavailable to any other person than the persons to whom it is addressed, or if it is an offer made to the company's existing shareholders or employees or to members of their families, it must be renounceable only to other persons who belong to those classes.[17]

Additionally, private companies' articles of association usually impose restrictions on the transferability of shares issued by them, even though there is no longer any legal requirement to this effect. The consequences of such restrictions and the limitations imposed by law on the offering of private companies' shares for subscription is that there is no active market in private companies' shares or debentures, and subscriptions for them have to be negotiated individually with investors. Although not subject to the legal restrictions which are imposed on private companies, the smaller public companies whose shares are not dealt in on any recognised market are in practice in much the same position.

Not surprisingly, the exclusion of private companies and the smaller public companies from the capital markets has in the past

[16] Companies Act 1985, s.89(1) to (3); s.91(1) and s.95(1) and (22).
[17] *Ibid.* s.60(1) to (5) and (7).

resulted in them being heavily dependent on bank finance to meet their cash needs in respect of current trading and for expansion. This situation has been somewhat alleviated in recent years by ordinary share capital being made available for well established or promising smaller companies by specialised investment and venture capital companies, such as Investors in Industry Group PLC and its subsidiaries. Also the specialised subsidiaries of the commercial banks have in recent years provided venture capital for such companies by subscribing for their shares and convertible debentures. As an alternative, smaller public and private companies may seek to raise venture capital from private investors who avail themselves of the personal tax advantages offered by the Business Expansion Scheme. This is an area of financing which is ripe for expansion, and one where increased investment activity will be essential if there is to be a lasting national economic revival after the years of recession.

3. THE FUTURE—A PROGNOSIS

This book has surveyed the recent developments in basic banking facilities for financing companies and their operations, has looked at the specialised forms which bank financing of companies can take, and has charted the present frontier between the provision of finance for companies by banks and by other institutions which may be, but are not necessarily, connected with banks at all. It now remains to draw the lines of development together, to envisage how banking services may be enlarged or elaborated over the next few years, and how banks may undertake financing activities which at present are largely left to other institutions. It is certain that the momentum of change will not slacken, and that with the increasing number of financial conglomerates, that is groups of companies whose specialised subsidiaries provide a wide range of financial services, the pace of change is likely to become faster.

There are three areas of financial activity where during the next few years banks are most likely to diversify the present forms of financial assistance which they provide for companies. The first of these is the provision of finance for small and medium-sized companies on terms which are more suited to their needs and their own rate of growth than the traditional overdraft facility and the term loan. The second is the provision of finance for large and medium-sized companies in ways which involve the banks taking an equity interest, or at least a conditional or limited equity interest, in the companies' business ventures, or even in their whole business undertakings. The third area for likely expansion is the provision of finance for companies under arrangements by which the investing public is invited to participate in the benefits and the risks, so that the banks may arrange for larger amounts of capital to be made available because of their own diminished participation in each arrangement. This may enable the banks to provide and raise loans for companies on terms which match their needs more closely than the existing standard conditions of long-term bank loans.

(1) *Finance for small and medium-sized companies*

Small and even medium-sized companies which do not qualify for, or do not want, an admission of their securities to dealings on the Stock Exchange, have a continuing need for medium and long term financing beyond that provided by the bank overdraft or short term loan. This has been emphasised repeatedly by the Macmillan Committee in 1931, the Radcliffe Committee in 1959, the Bolton Committee in 1971 and the Wilson Committee in 1980, and the limited availability of suitable forms of long-term finance for them has long been known as the Macmillan Gap or the equity gap. Banks have made some move toward bridging the gap by extending the duration of the term loans they make to small companies so as to relieve them from the constant awareness that a reversal in their fortunes, even though temporary and not radical, may result in the calling in of their bank overdrafts or loans at a time when they are least able to repay or to raise funds elsewhere. The small company sector has received more help in this respect, however, from the specialised institutions which have been set up (sometimes with the collaboration of the banks) to make long term loans to small companies and, more importantly, to take equity participations in them on the basis that the existing management of the company is left intact, but subject to a degree of surveillance by the investing institutions. The banks themselves have set up wholly-owned subsidiaries in recent years to invest in small and medium-sized companies which have sound trading records or good prospects, but these venture capital subsidiaries have not yet invested extensively in the equity shares of small companies, although they have taken substantial holdings in medium-sized concerns.

(2) *Buy-outs and buy-ins*

One of the situations where the banks have proved more ready to provide finance for small companies by taking equity participations has been where the management of the company offers to buy out the existing shareholders of a company for which an outside take-over bid has been made, or which is threatened with closure. The management makes its offer to acquire the other shareholders' holdings so as to retain control of the company in its own hands, but is rarely able to find the money needed to buy out those holdings, and is therefore compelled to look to banks, investment trust companies and venture capital companies to provide the money needed. Much of this money has in the past been provided by way of loan, but too high a ratio between the money borrowed to acquire outside shareholders' holdings and the share capital invested in the company can cause difficulties in the future for the company and its management. This can only be avoided by a substantial part of the finance provided by banks and other institutions taking the form of equity capital. The venture capital subsidiaries of banks have recently become increasingly willing to match loans made by their parent banks in this situation by subscribing for new equity capital of companies whose managements intend to buy out the other existing shareholders, but often only on condition that the management of the company can be called on to purchase the shares subscribed for at pre-agreed prices after a certain length of time, or if certain adverse developments take place, or if the company does not attain the level of turnover or profits which the venture capital company requires.

Another situation where the venture capital subsidiaries of banks have in recent years been willing to take equity participations in small companies, often in conjunction with loans made by the parent banks of the venture capital companies, has been when a larger company or companies were also taking substantial equity participations as well. The motives of the larger companies in doing this are various, ranging from the desire to use the small company as a supplier of products or components which the larger companies need, to an intention to develop the small company as a specialist manufacturer or supplier of goods or services which will require more capital to exploit its speciality than its present management can provide. In such a buy-in operation the bank acts as a supportive associate of the larger company or companies, and the equity participation of the bank's venture capital subsidiary in the small company's equity is always a minor one compared with that of the larger company or companies. Moreover, and this is perhaps the most significant feature of such arrangements, the loan made by the bank to the small company is usually very much larger than the equity participation by its venture capital subsidiary, and the loan is guaranteed by the larger company or companies.

(3) *Potentiality for development*

These examples of equity investment by banking groups indicate how the acquisition of equity participations in smaller companies by banks and their subsidiaries may increase in future. The need of such companies for finance will arise in novel situations, and because of certain attractive features in those situations, banks or their subsidiaries will invest. This will then be repeated in respect of other small companies, and it will quickly be accepted as normal for banks generally to participate by taking a minor or substantial equity participation in situations of that kind. Eventually these special situations will become so multifarious that banks will accept it as normal for them to take equity participations in small companies because of the needs of the particular company, and not because its situation fits into a pre-ordained mould. In other words, the special situations will merge and become general. How long it will take for this to happen is very much a matter of conjecture, but eventually it is certain to come about.

Financing medium-sized and large companies on an equity basis

Banks are unlikely to invest in the ordinary shares of larger companies extensively, or otherwise than through their merchant banking subsidiaries which have the larger companies as clients. This is because the means by which such companies will be able to raise equity capital through the markets for securities without resorting to the banks will become easier in the future with the availability of increasing volumes of funds seeking investments. Nevertheless, it is likely during the coming years that banks will provide loan finance for larger companies on terms which are similar in important respects to those on which equity shareholders participate in the companies' earnings and growth.

The forerunner of this development is, of course, the bank project loan which is convertible at the option of the borrowing company into a non-recourse loan on the successful completion of the project. A project loan is susceptible to this treatment only if it is made to finance an operation resulting in the creation of a capital asset which will be income-producing for an extended period of time, such as an oilfield, a port or airport or a fully developed or redeveloped urban complex of offices, residences and light engineering factories which are let at commercial rents. At present such convertible project loans are made on terms that if the conversion option is exercised by the company, the bank receives a higher rate of interest than it did while the project was being carried out, but the bank can look only to the future income of the completed project and the assets comprised in the project for its increased interest payments and to the repayment of the principal of the loan. The amount of income which is annually appropriated to satisfying the bank's claims is made proportionate to the income yielded each year by the completed project, the rate of amortisation of the initial capital value of the completed project and the amount of principal which remains owing to the bank. If the income appropriated to the bank proves insufficient to repay the principal in full or to pay the higher rate of interest after the conversion of the loan, the bank cannot recover the whole or any part of the deficiency from the borrowing company, unless it expressly agrees to be responsible for it.

The converted project loan is a formal embodiment of the modern banking principle that in negotiating a loan it is more important to forecast accurately the future cash flow from the asset whose acquisition or construction the loan will finance than to value the present market value of that asset correctly. Nevertheless, a convertible non-

115

recourse project loan is still a loan with an equity or risk element added, and not a true equity participation in the borrowing company. The bank is dependent after the conversion of the loan on the level of income yielded by the completed project (together with the assets comprised in it) for repayment of the principal of its loan and the payment of current interest, but the bank ensures that it has a first charge on that income to satisfy its claims, and that the forecast income under even adverse conditions should be adequate to satisfy those claims twice or more times over.

The convertible project loan, however, does set a pattern for future developments which could result in banks making loans on real equity terms, for example, by the company contracting to pay the bank a rate of interest which varies with the level of income from the completed project, or a higher rate of interest some part of which will be deferred or capitalised if the annual income from the project falls short of a certain figure, or a percentage of the annual income instead of interest with or without provision for a variation of the percentage depending on the level of income. An equity basis for the repayment of the principal of the loan could also be introduced by scaling down the percentage of it which has to be repaid if the total income from the completed project is less than a certain amount, or probably more acceptable to the banks, by deferring the repayment dates if the total income does not attain a certain level within an agreed period. Such arrangements could be made very attractive to banks, and could be proposed to them as an alternative to a term loan at a fixed rate of interest or a rate which is variable only with the market level of interest rates. The greater the equity element in such arrangements, the greater the risk to the banks would be, of course, but it is not beyond possibility that within a few years banks will find such risks acceptable if the borrower is a large and financially sound company.

Securitisation and investor participation in bank financing

The third and final development in methods of bank financing which can be envisaged as likely over the next few years is the adaptation of a practice which some banks have recently employed to dispose of their rights under certain loans they have already made, particularly certain sovereign loans, so as to replenish their resources with the proceeds of the disposal and so enable themselves to make new loans on more advantageous or secure terms. These disposals have been carried out by the disposing bank transfering its rights under the original loans, whether syndicated or not, to trustees as a package and assigning the bank's beneficial interest in the package in shares to several other banks, mainly overseas banks, so that each of the purchasing banks acquires a *pro rata* equitable interest in the whole package. The loans are, of course, disposed of in this way at a price equal to the purchasing banks' respective percentage shares of the current market value of the package of loans, and the proceeds received by the disposing bank are added to the funds it has available for re-lending or reinvestment.

Some building societies are proposing to dispose in much the same way of their rights under mortgages they have taken from house purchasers. The selected mortgages will be packaged so as to constitute a trust fund, and shares in the fund will be offered to institutional and other investors at prices reflecting the current market value of the mortgages. This method of refinancing mortgage loans has been used by the German land mortgage banks (*Hypothekenbanken*) for over 100 years, and the securities issued by those banks each represent a share in a package of mortgages held by the issuing bank and are themselves marketable securities known as pledged mortgage bonds (*Hypothekenpfandbriefe*). The same idea of packaging investments into a fund and disposing of shares in the fund to investors also, of course, underlies the British unit trust. The process has recently come to be known by the singularly unattractive name of "securitisation."

An obvious candidate for securitisation is a package of term loans, project finance loans or other forms of medium or long-term advances made by a bank. The package would have a readily ascertainable market value, and shares in the package could be sold by the lending bank or, if the loans were syndicated, by all the lending banks acting together, to institutional or other investors at a price which reflected that market value. The investors would acquire fractional interests in a portfolio of good quality loans, and the fact that the bank or banks concerned had made the loans in the first place after making the normal enquiries about the borrowers, and had since monitored the borrowers' behaviour, would provide investors with some assurance as to the quality of the loans. This could be strengthened by appropriate warranties given by the bank or banks that payments under the loans had been made in full to date and that these had been no defaults by the borrowers, and where necessary, the bank or banks could give guarantees for the repayment with interest of a certain fraction of the amounts outstanding under the loans. By marketing loan portfolios in this way banks would increase their own liquidity and consequently their ability to make fresh loans to new borrowers.

Whether banks will avail themselves of their ability to mobilise medium and long-term loans which they have made remains to be seen, as does the size and nature of the market in which such securitisation operations are carried out. Like the other possible developments in the forms of bank financing which have been considered in this Chapter, the seeds of the development already exist and have already been planted, if only on a tentative or experimental basis. Their growth of such new ways of financing companies to full stature

117

and the realisation of the potential benefits they offer for both banks and companies will depend partly on market forces, partly on the financial needs of companies and partly on the willingness of banks to innovate.